Withdrawn

L. Frank Baum

WHO WROTE THAT?

WHO WROTE THAT?

L. Frank Baum

Dennis Abrams

**Foreword by
Kyle Zimmer**

CHELSEA HOUSE
PUBLISHERS
An imprint of Infobase Publishing

L. Frank Baum

Chelsea House
An imprint of Infobase Publishing
132 West 31st Street
New York, NY 10001

Library of Congress Cataloging-in-Publication Data
Abrams, Dennis, 1960-
 L. Frank Baum / Dennis Abrams.
 p. cm. — (Who wrote that?)
 Includes bibliographical references and index.
 ISBN 978-1-60413-501-5 (hardcover : acid-free paper) 1. Baum, L. Frank
(Lyman Frank), 1856-1919—Juvenile literature. 2. Authors, American—20th
century—Biography—Juvenile literature. 3. Children's stories—Authorship—
Juvenile literature. 4. Baum, L. Frank (Lyman Frank), 1856-1919. Wizard of Oz—
Juvenile literature. I. Title. II. Series.
 PS3503.A923Z55 2010
 813'.4—dc22
 [B]   2009022337

Chelsea House books are available at special discounts when purchased in bulk quantities for business, associations, institutions, or sales promotions. Please call our Special Sales Department in New York at (212) 967-8800 or (800) 322-8755.

You can find Chelsea House on the World Wide Web at http://www.chelseahouse.com.

Text design by Keith Trego and Erika K. Arroyo
Cover design by Alicia Post
Composition by EJB Publishing Services
Cover printed by Bang Printing, Brainerd, MN
Book printed and bound by Bang Printing, Brainerd, MN
Date printed: April 2010
Printed in the United States of America

10 9 8 7 6 5 4 3 2 1

This book is printed on acid-free paper.

All links and Web addresses were checked and verified to be correct at the time of publication. Because of the dynamic nature of the Web, some addresses and links may have changed since publication and may no longer be valid.

Table of Contents

FOREWORD BY
KYLE ZIMMER
PRESIDENT, FIRST BOOK

HUMANITY IS POWERED by stories. From our earliest days as thinking beings, we employed every available tool to tell each other stories. We danced, drew pictures on the walls of our caves, spoke, and sang. All of this extraordinary effort was designed to entertain, recount the news of the day, explain natural occurrences—and then gradually to build religious and cultural traditions and establish the common bonds and continuity that eventually formed civilizations. Stories are the most powerful force in the universe; they are the primary element that has distinguished our evolutionary path.

Our love of the story has not diminished with time. Enormous segments of societies are devoted to the art of storytelling. Book sales in the United States alone topped $24 billion in 2006; movie studios spend fortunes to create and promote stories; and the news industry is more pervasive in its presence than ever before.

There is no mystery to our fascination. Great stories are magic. They can introduce us to new cultures, or remind us of the nobility and failures of our own, inspire us to greatness or scare us to death; but above all, stories provide human insight on a level that is unavailable through any other source. In fact, stories connect each of us to the rest of humanity not just in our own time, but also throughout history.

This special magic of books is the greatest treasure that we can hand down from generation to generation. In fact, that spark in a child that comes from books became the motivation for the creation of my organization, First Book, a national literacy program with a simple mission: to provide new books to the most disadvantaged children. At present, First Book has been at work in hundreds of communities for over a decade. Every year children in need receive millions of books through our organization and millions more are provided through dedicated literacy institutions across the United States and around the world. In addition, groups of people dedicate themselves tirelessly to working with children to share reading and stories in every imaginable setting from schools to the streets. Of course, this Herculean effort serves many important goals. Literacy translates to productivity and employability in life and many other valid and even essential elements. But at the heart of this movement are people who love stories, love to read, and want desperately to ensure that no one misses the wonderful possibilities that reading provides.

When thinking about the importance of books, there is an overwhelming urge to cite the literary devotion of great minds. Some have written of the magnitude of the importance of literature. Amy Lowell, an American poet, captured the concept when she said, "Books are more than books. They are the life, the very heart and core of ages past, the reason why men lived and worked and died, the essence and quintessence of their lives." Others have spoken of their personal obsession with books, as in Thomas Jefferson's simple statement: "I live for books." But more compelling, perhaps, is the almost instinctive excitement in children for books and stories.

Throughout my years at First Book, I have heard truly extraordinary stories about the power of books in the lives of children. In one case, a homeless child, who had been bounced from one location to another, later resurfaced— and the only possession that he had fought to keep was the book he was given as part of a First Book distribution months earlier. More recently, I met a child who, upon receiving the book he wanted, flashed a big smile and said, "This is my big chance!" These snapshots reveal the true power of books and stories to give hope and change lives.

As these children grow up and continue to develop their love of reading, they will owe a profound debt to those volunteers who reached out to them—a debt that they may repay by reaching out to spark the next generation of readers. But there is a greater debt owed by all of us—a debt to the storytellers, the authors, who have bound us together, inspired our leaders, fueled our civilizations, and helped us put our children to sleep with their heads full of images and ideas.

WHO WROTE THAT? is a series of books dedicated to introducing us to a few of these incredible individuals. While we have almost always honored stories, we have not uniformly honored storytellers. In fact, some of the most important authors have toiled in complete obscurity throughout their lives or have been openly persecuted for the uncomfortable truths that they have laid before us. When confronted with the magnitude of their written work or perhaps the daily grind of our own, we can forget that writers are people. They struggle through the same daily indignities and dental appointments, and they experience the intense joy and bottomless despair that many of us do. Yet somehow they rise above it all to deliver a powerful thread that connects us all. It is a rare honor to have the opportunity that these books provide to share the lives of these extraordinary people. Enjoy.

L. Frank Baum, creator of the Oz series and many other fantasy works, is photographed circa 1908, a few years after becoming a full-time writer.

1

A Startling Coincidence

ON DECEMBER 21, 1937, Walt Disney Productions premiered the first feature-length animated film, *Snow White and the Seven Dwarfs*. The film was an immediate box-office sensation. It made more money than any film in 1938, briefly becoming the highest-grossing film in American history; it also became the first movie to have a soundtrack recording released for it. Needless to say, every other studio in Hollywood was soon on the lookout for its own version of *Snow White*—a children's film that would be a guaranteed moneymaker.

For Metro-Goldwyn-Mayer Studios (MGM), the decision of what film to make was obvious. In 1934, Goldwyn Studios had purchased the right to make a film of L. Frank Baum's classic novel *The Wonderful Wizard of Oz*, an enormously popular American children's book since its publication in 1900, for just $40,000. The studio, however, lacked the resources to film it properly and did nothing. Four years later, MGM, Hollywood's richest and most successful studio, purchased the rights from Goldwyn Studios for $75,000 and set out to make a spectacular film that, while not animated, would rival anything that Disney could do.

With a budget of more than $2 million, more costly than any other film MGM was making that year, the studio was obviously willing to spare no expense to make Baum's fantasy world come to life on the big screen. Elaborate sets were built, screenplay writers went to work to make a script from Baum's novel, and casting began in earnest.

Judy Garland was picked to play Baum's heroine, Dorothy Gale. Ray Bolger was selected to play the Scarecrow, and Bert Lahr would play the Cowardly Lion. Jack Haley was to play the Tin Woodman after the studio's original choice, Buddy Ebsen, was forced to drop out after inhaling the aluminum powder that had been tested for use as his makeup. (After that mishap, the studio switched to aluminum paste to create the Tin Man's metallic look.) Margaret Hamilton would become the film's villainess, the Wicked Witch of the West. And finally, beloved character actor Frank Morgan would play the film's title role, the Wizard of Oz.

Actually, Morgan played *five* roles in the film: the Emerald City cabby who drove the Horse-of-a-Different Color; a guard at the entrance to the Wizard's palace; the doorkeeper at the Wizard's palace; the Great and Powerful Wizard of

Oz himself; and finally, a role that was not even in the book—the carnival con man, Professor Marvel.

Naturally, completely different costumes and makeup were needed for each of these roles. Fortunately for Morgan, since the portions of the film in which he appeared were the last to be filmed, the studio had time to determine just the right look for each character. Still, even though Morgan did not make his first appearance in front of a camera until January 14, 1939, he began posing for makeup and costume test shots for all of his characters two months earlier, in mid-November of 1938.

It was on November 17, 1938, that Morgan first tested his Professor Marvel makeup on the set, using the same costume he had used for his Wizard test shots one day earlier. Six days later, Morgan once again posed for Professor Marvel test shots, but this time with a different hairstyle, tie, and jacket. It is the story behind this jacket that is one of the oddest coincidences in film history and certainly an appropriate addition to the legend of Oz.

Aljean Harmetz related the story in her book, *The Making of the Wizard of Oz*:

> What definitely did occur on *The Wizard of Oz*—perhaps the most astonishing thing that did occur—was dismissed as a publicity stunt. Yet it is vouched for by [cinematographer] Hal Rossen and his niece Helene Bowman and by Mary Mayer, who served briefly as the unit publicist on the picture. "For Professor Marvel's coat," says Mary Mayer, "they wanted grandeur gone to seed. A nice-looking coat but very tattered. So the wardrobe department went down to an old second-hand store on Main Street and bought a whole rack of coats.

In this cast photo from The Wizard of Oz *(1939), shown clockwise from upper left are Frank Morgan (as Professor Marvel), Charley Grapewin (as Uncle Henry), Bert Lahr (as Zeke), Clara Blandick (as Auntie Em), Jack Haley (as Hickory), Ray Bolger (as Hunk), and Judy Garland (as Dorothy Gale). Morgan is wearing L. Frank Baum's old coat.*

And Frank Morgan and the wardrobe man and [director] Victor Fleming got together and chose one. It was kind of a Prince Albert coat. It was black broadcloth and it had a velvet collar, but the nap was all worn off the velvet." Helene Bowman recalls the coat as "ratty with age, a Prince Albert jacket with a green look."

The coat had the right look of shabby gentility, and one hot afternoon Frank Morgan turned out the pocket. Inside was the name "L. Frank Baum."

"We wired the tailor in Chicago," says Mary Mayer, "and sent pictures. And the tailor sent back a notarized letter saying that the coat had been made for Frank Baum. Baum's widow identified the coat, too, and after the picture was finished we presented it to her. But I could never get anyone to believe the story.[1]

Who would believe such a story? What are the odds that a worn, secondhand jacket once owned by L. Frank Baum, the creator of Oz, would, many years later, become part of the costume for a character in a film based on his book? If you read about it in a novel, you would have a hard time believing it.

Yet, it seems somewhat right that it did actually happen, for Baum's life itself was riddled with those same kinds of

Did you know...

Before MGM made its classic 1939 film, *The Wizard of Oz*, numerous other film-makers had tried to bring Baum's novel *The Wonderful Wizard of Oz* to life on the big screen. Perhaps one of the oddest versions is the 1925 silent film *The Wizard of Oz*. The plot is barely recognizable as Baum's: Dorothy is really the Princess Dorothea of Oz, two Kansas farmhands disguise themselves as a scarecrow and a tin woodman, and the tin woodman himself becomes the story's villain. Interestingly, the role of the tin woodman is played by Oliver Hardy, who just a year later would achieve cinematic immortality as one half of the comedy team of Laurel and Hardy.

improbabilities. A child of wealth, he struggled for long periods of his life just to make a living. A man of poor health, he was a tireless worker, always eager to try something new. A man who became one of the most popular American children's book authors, he did not even publish his first book until he was in his forties. A man whose literary masterpiece, *The Wonderful Wizard of Oz*, described by author Michael O. Riley as "the quintessential American fairy tale,"[2] was, by the 1950s, dismissed by both American critics and librarians as being the author of badly written, sensational, and even politically suspect children's books!

Novelist Alison Lurie, who has also written a number of highly regarded nonfiction books on children's literature, described the phenomenon in a 1974 essay in the *New York Review of Books*:

> For more than half a century after L. Frank Baum discovered it in 1900, the Land of Oz had a curious reputation. American children by the thousands went there happily every year, but authorities in the field of juvenile literature, like suspicious and conservative travel agents, refused to recommend it or even to handle tickets. Librarians would not buy the Oz books, schoolteachers would not let you write reports on them, and the best-known history of children's books made no reference to their existence.[3]

Indeed, it was up to writer Martin Gardner to begin the first steps in restoring Baum's tattered literary reputation. His 1957 essay "The Royal Historian of Oz" began by stating:

> America's greatest writer of children's fantasy was, as everyone knows except librarians and critics of juvenile literature, L. Frank Baum. His [The] *Wonderful Wizard of Oz* has long

been the nation's best known, best loved native fairy tale, but you will look in vain for any recognition of this fact in recent histories of children's books. . . . No one has felt it worth while to inquire as to what merits the Oz books may have or what manner of man it was who first produced them. By and large, the critics have looked upon Baum's writing as tawdry popular writing. . . . Fortunately, children themselves seldom listen to such learned opinion . . . children still turn the pages of Baum's Oz books with passionate delight.[4]

Even today, more than 50 years after Gardner's defense, Baum is still best known by most people for only his first Oz book, the one that inspired *The Wizard of Oz*, one of the most popular films ever made. Yet *The Wonderful Wizard of Oz* was just the first in a series of 14 books about Oz—a series that creates an alternate world as complete and magical as any in children's literature. L. Frank Baum was also the author of more than 41 "non-Oz" novels, 82 short stories, and more than 200 poems, many of which are worthy of rediscovery. On top of that, did you know that he was also a successful playwright? A successful actor? A businessman, traveling salesman, pioneering moviemaker, newspaper editor, and exotic poultry breeder?

Baum's life spanned the last half of the nineteenth century and the first quarter of the twentieth. In search of his calling, Baum traveled from the oil fields of Pennsylvania to the frontiers of the Dakota Territory, from the booming metropolis of Chicago to a Hollywood in its infancy as the moviemaking capital of the world. Baum's life is the kind of tale storytellers dream of. It is through his life and travels that we will, as Martin Gardner put it, "inquire as to what merits the Oz books may have or what manner of man it was who first produced them."[5]

The Cardiff Giant dwarfs the workers who dug him out of his "grave" in Cardiff, New York, in 1869. By the time the giant was declared a fake, the bogus behemoth had become a sensation that swept the country. A young L. Frank Baum poked fun at the giant in his Rose Lawn Home Journal.

2

A Young Man of Many Interests

LYMAN FRANK BAUM was born on May 15, 1856, in Chittenango, New York, about 15 miles east of Syracuse, the seventh of nine children born to Benjamin Ward and Cynthia Stanton Baum. As was common in those days, four of the Baums' children died in infancy. It was, in that way and many others, a very different world than the one we live in today.

When Baum was born, the United States of America was still half slave and half free; the Civil War was still five years away. Most of the technology we take for granted today had not yet been invented. And, curiously, even the idea of "childhood" as we understand it now was very different. Children, for the most part, were not considered to be in need of special care and education. In many ways, they were thought of as "miniature adults" and were treated as such and put out to work as quickly as possible. That, however, was about to change.

As author Gore Vidal pointed out in his 1977 essay on L. Frank Baum, "The Oz Books," the year 1856 was the beginning of a new attitude toward children and their needs:

> [In] 1856 a number of interesting things happened in the United States. Mrs. Carl Schurz opened the first kindergarten at Watertown, Wisconsin. In Chelsea, Massachusetts, the Universalist Church observed, for the first time anywhere, Children's Day. In New York City the big theatrical hit of the season was a pantomime (from London) called *Planche, or Lively Fairies*. The year's most successful book of poems was J.G. Whittier's *The Panorama and Other Poems*, a volume that included "The Barefoot Boy." People were unexpectedly interested in the care, education, and comfort of children. It is somehow both fitting and satisfying that on May 15 of the first American Children's Year Lyman Frank Baum was born.[1]

EARLY CHILDHOOD

Baum's father, Benjamin, the son of a German emigrant, began work as a barrel maker at a young age. He married Cynthia Stanton, the daughter of a successful farmer, in 1842 and set out to make his fortune as a businessman. Although he was not always successful, by constantly trying new things, he managed to first survive and then prosper. By 1850, he was a partner in a pumpkin-vending business with his wife's brother, as well as a manufacturer of butter and cheese.

In 1854, the Baums moved to Chittenango, already the home of Benjamin's sister and parents. Benjamin bought land there, where he built both the family house as well as a barrel factory. By 1860, Benjamin's real estate holdings were valued at $6,000—a sizeable amount of money at the time. But barrels and dairy products were just the start of Benjamin Baum's fortune.

In 1859, oil was discovered in Titusville, Pennsylvania, located just 200 miles from Syracuse. Benjamin Baum was quick to see the financial opportunity. He began purchasing oil fields and bought enough land between Bradford, Pennsylvania, and Olean, New York, to develop the entire town of Gilmour, along with its hotel and opera house. By 1860, Baum's fortunes had grown to such a point that he could move his family to an even larger house in Syracuse. In order to ensure his continued financial success, he kept his hand in many financial pots: Baum had enormous real estate holdings, traded stocks (and even had an office in New York City), established the Second National Bank in Syracuse, and helped organize Neal, Baum & Company, Wholesale Dry Goods.

The onetime barrel maker was now able to provide his family with nearly anything they desired. In 1866, when L. Frank Baum was 10 years old, the family moved to a country estate north of Syracuse that Cynthia named Rose Lawn in honor of the hundreds of rosebushes that grew there. Although the house did not have running water, it was an ideal place for young Frank (who had already stopped using his much-hated first name "Lyman") to live in. Many years later, he used his memories of his home in his book *Dot and Tot of Merryland*:

> The cool but sun-kissed mansion . . . was built in a quaint yet pretty fashion, with many wings and gables and broad verandas on every side. Before it were acres and acres of velvety

green lawn, sprinkled with shrubbery and dotted with beds of bright flowers. In every direction were winding paths, covered with white gravel, which led to all parts, looking for all the world like a map.[2]

But even the family's wealth could not guarantee young Frank Baum's happiness. Due to a defective heart, Frank was in poor health a great deal of the time during his childhood. Whether he was born with the heart condition or it was the result of a case of rheumatic fever is unknown. In a case such as his, the patient often grows out of the disease but is left with damaged heart valves. Over time, this condition leads to further health problems between the ages of 40 and 60. Baum, after suffering as a child, recovered and enjoyed generally good health for most of his adult life, with the exception of severe heart pains after serious exertion, before his condition returned when he was in his fifties.

Because of his illness, Frank spent little time in typical roughhouse play with his brothers and sisters. Instead, he kept largely to himself, reading and daydreaming his days away. Like the rest of the Baum children, Frank was home-schooled until the age of 12 and rarely left the confines of his family's house and gardens. But it was then, after his doctor agreed that he was healthy enough, that his parents decided to send him to study at Peekskill Military Academy, perhaps in an effort to toughen him up.

In hindsight, it was an obvious mistake to send this weak-hearted dreamy boy to live in a military academy. Miserable in such a tough, regimented environment, Frank sent a constant stream of letters home to his father complaining about the sadistic treatment he received there. He claimed that his teachers "were heartless, callous and continually indulging in petty nagging . . . about as human as a school of fish . . . [and] were quick to slap a boy in the face [if he] violated in the slightest way any of the strict and often unreasonable rules."[3]

Frank survived there for two dismal years. But one day, when he was severely reprimanded for gazing out of his classroom windows at the birds when he was *supposed* to be studying, he suffered a heart attack. Needless to say, Baum was quickly removed from the Peekskill Military Academy. His further education would be at home, where he received private tutoring. He also developed an insatiable thirst for literature, educating himself by reading the novels of Charles Dickens, William Makepeace Thackeray, and Charles Reade—works that were new at the time but have since become classics of English literature.

Not surprisingly, given the books he was to write later in life, he also enjoyed reading fairy tales. Years later, he recalled: "I demanded fairy stories when I was a youngster . . . and I was a critical reader too. One thing I never liked then, and that was the introduction of witches and goblins into the story. I didn't like the little dwarfs in the woods bobbing up with their horrors."[4]

FROM READING TO WRITING

When Frank was 14 years old and bored during a visit to his father's Syracuse office, he wandered away and discovered a small printing office. It was love at first sight. Frank was mesmerized watching the printer at work and decided on the spot that he wanted to become either a printer or a newspaperman. Fortunately, his father was in a position that allowed him to cultivate his son's career dreams. He bought his son a small printing press of his own, along with all the equipment necessary to go right to work. After Frank and his younger brother Harry learned how to work the machine, the pair decided to print their own monthly newspaper.

It was called the *Rose Lawn Home Journal*. A total of five issues were printed. They included work by Frank and other members of his family, as well as pieces taken from national magazines and books. They published poetry, such as,

> Father, mother, sister, me,
>
> We're run over—here we be.
>
> The engine was old; the boiler rusted,
>
> And all of a sudden the darn thing busted!![5]

Owning a printing press also allowed Frank and Harry to earn an income by printing signs, stationary, and handbills, the majority of which were done for their uncle's firm. By 1873, the boys had done well enough that they could afford to purchase a new, higher-quality press!

Other interests soon followed. When Frank took up stamp collecting, he also published a journal, *The Stamp Collector*, which included reviews of the latest stamps, as well as articles discussing issues in the field of stamp collecting.

He also published the 11-page *Baum's Complete Stamp Dealers' Directory* and teamed up with a traveling salesman named William Norris to form a mail-order business in foreign postage stamps. The *Directory* included advertisements not only for the mail-order business (Baum, Norris and Company, Importing Dealers in Foreign Stamps) but for his printing company, the Young American Job Printing Press, as well as for *The Empire*, a "First Class Monthly Amateur Paper," published by Baum and a new business partner, Thomas G. Alford Jr., the son of New York's lieutenant governor. Frank Baum was just 17 years old.

If that was not enough, Frank soon developed a new interest, one that would claim him for the rest of his life. Benjamin Baum, always eager to expand his business

Did you know...

In the July 1, 1871 issue of the *Rose Lawn Home Journal*, Baum made fun of the recent discovery of the Cardiff Giant.

What was the Cardiff Giant? On a farm only about eight miles from the Baums', about one year earlier, a local con artist had buried a ten-and-a-half-foot-tall statue of a man. When it was discovered by workmen a year later, many people thought that it was a petrified man descended from the race of giants described in the Bible, possibly left behind by the Great Flood.

The find became a major tourist attraction. Even legendary showman P.T. Barnum got into the act, creating his own version of the giant and calling the original giant a fake! The original giant is currently on display at the Farmer's Museum at Cooperstown, New York; Barnum's copy is on display at Marvin's Marvelous Mechanical Museum in Farmington Hills, Michigan. And, not surprisingly at all, it was the brouhaha over the two giants that led to the immortal words, "There's a sucker born every minute."

interests, had purchased a string of small theaters in New York and Pennsylvania. Frank visited them as often as he could, enthralled by the stage, the actors, the whole magic of theater. He decided that the theater life was for him and that he would become an actor.

But without experience, he found that no theater company was willing to hire him. Finally, the manager of a traveling Shakespearean troupe claimed to see promise in the handsome yet inexperienced actor and agreed to hire him on one condition. Frank would have to furnish his own complete set of costumes for every conceivable role he might play before he could join the company.

Frank went to his parents to get the money necessary to have the costumes made. Although somewhat skeptical, his doting parents agreed to pay for the costumes, but with one condition of their own. Frank would have to take a stage name since the family name had become highly respected in the community. Frank agreed, and thousands of dollars' worth of costumes later, the newly named actor George Brooks joined the company.

Their first stop was Oneida, New York, where "Brooks" was told to arrive at the theater one hour before curtain. As Frank settled into his dressing room, an actor came in who said that he was to play Romeo, but his doublet was torn. He asked to borrow one of Frank's costumes. One actor after another came into Frank's dressing room to "borrow" a costume. In just a few days, all of the costumes had been borrowed, none had been returned, and Frank was forced to return home with his tail between his legs. Temporarily turning his back on the theater, he went to work at his brother-in-law's wholesale dry-goods store, Neal, Baum & Company, in Syracuse.

CHICKENS

After learning the ins and outs of the dry-goods business, Frank went to the family's farm to learn the agricultural business. Adjoining Rose Lawn, Spring Farm boasted 80 acres of dairy land, as well as a 160-acre commercial grain and livestock farm. It was here that Frank had seen his first scarecrow as a boy. Even then, he saw scarecrows as more than just clothes stuffed with straw, telling a reporter in 1904: "They always seemed to my childish imagination as just about to wave their arms, straighten up and stalk across the field on their long legs."[6] Not all of his childhood impressions of scarecrows were so innocent. As a young boy, he often had nightmares in which he was chased by a scarecrow that disintegrated into a pile of straw just moments before catching him.

But now, as a young man learning the family business at Spring Farm, Baum found himself with yet another new interest: fancy poultry breeding. Never one to do anything halfheartedly, he formed a new company, B.W. Baum & Sons, with his father and his brother Harry, and went to work raising Hamburgs, rare black chickens with varied secondary colorings. After he helped found the Empire State Poultry Association in 1878, his chickens began to win prizes. He was so successful, in fact, that when he attended the Seventh Annual Meeting of the American Poultry Association in Indianapolis, Indiana, in January 1880, he was promptly elected to its executive committee!

And, of course, since Frank was interested in poultry, he also began *writing* about poultry. In March 1880, he founded *The Poultry Record*, a monthly trade journal. Although much of the copy and pictures were taken from rival journals, he did write the editorials himself, in which he "expressed bold opinions on the fancy chicken trade,"[7] while occasionally mocking the foibles of rival breeders. After just a few issues, Baum grew tired of the grind of producing a journal each month and sold the paper to the *New York Farmer and Dairyman*, while continuing to write his monthly column, "The Poultry Yard."

Baum's interest in poultry continued, however. In May 1881, the publisher of the industry's leading journal, *The Poultry World*, commissioned Baum to write a long article on Hamburgs that was serialized in the magazine from July to November 1882. The series was so successful that, without Baum's knowledge, the articles were reprinted in book form as *The Book of the Hamburgs, A Brief Treatise upon the Mating, Rearing, and Management of the Different Varieties of Hamburgs*. It was L. Frank Baum's first book.

Although the book is a technical manual targeted at breeders of fancy poultry, Baum's prose still hints at the writer to come. Describing a Hamburg mother hen in the most loving of terms, for example, he lays the groundwork for his descriptions of Billina, the talking hen introduced in *Ozma of Oz*:

> For the first week, perhaps nearly every old hen is faithful to her little brood, and guards them with that maternal tenderness for which she has been made the symbol of motherly love. But this care soon wearies her, and in a few days she begins to neglect them, marching around in the chill and drenching rains of spring, and dragging her little brood after her through the damp grass, entirely oblivious of their sufferings; and one by one they drop off.[8]

Baum maintained his love of chickens throughout his life, even raising a flock of Rhode Island Reds in his Hollywood home, Ozcot. Still, there was one thing that the young Baum loved even more than poultry: the stage. And, despite his earlier bad experience, he was determined to give acting another try.

Maud Gage Baum had an abiding faith in her husband's abilities, even in the early years of their marriage when he was a struggling actor and playwright with just a few titles to his credit. They would remain devoted to each other until Baum's death in 1919.

3

Trying to
Find His Way

DURING THIS PERIOD of his life, Baum managed to juggle several careers at once. In 1878, while still in the process of developing his love of fancy poultry, he joined the Union Square Theatre in New York. There, using the stage name Louis F. Baum, he appeared in a hit play *The Banker's Daughter*, which opened on November 30, 1878, and ran for 100 nights. It was his first stage success.

At the same time, he was also writing articles for the *New York Tribune* and landed a job as a reporter (through his father's influence) for the *Bradford Era*. But the theater was now his life. In 1880, Baum's father made him manager of the string of theaters that he owned in and around Bradford, Pennsylvania, and eventually gave him complete ownership.

When he had a difficult time finding theatrical companies willing to perform in small theaters in Pennsylvania oil towns, Baum started his own company that specialized in performing the plays of William Shakespeare. On one occasion, they were asked to give a performance of *Hamlet* in the town hall of a small oil settlement. When the company arrived at the hall, they were dismayed to find that there was no real stage, not even a raised platform.

Making do with what they could, Baum asked the oil workers to assemble a makeshift stage using planks precariously placed on top of wooden sawhorses. But since they refused to damage the planks by nailing them to the sawhorses, the stage had a tendency to wobble, and the actors had to move very, very carefully.

Naturally, Baum played the title role of Hamlet. In the scene in which Hamlet has to move backward upon seeing his father's ghost, Baum accidentally moved a plank out of place. The "ghost," covered with a white sheet as his costume and not able to see properly, promptly stepped into the hole that Baum caused and fell right through the stage. The oil workers thought that it was an intentional piece of comedy and laughed so hard that, according to Baum, "We had to repeat the scene five times before we could get on with the show."[1]

Baum took the opportunity of having his own theatrical company to write the kinds of plays that he hoped would be better suited to the taste of his working-class audiences than those of Shakespeare. He wrote three of them in 1882: *The Mackrummins* and *Matches*, both three-act comedy/dramas, and *The Maid of Arran*, a melodrama. (A melodrama is a stage, film, or television drama with generally stereotypical characters portraying big, over-the-top emotions in usually exaggerated dramatic situations.)

Of the three, it was *The Maid of Arran*, based on William Black's 1874 novel *A Princess of Thule,* that became a major hit. To adapt the novel into a play, Baum moved the story's location from Scotland to Ireland, cut out the comedy, made the story more melodramatic, and added songs. The play seemed to match the tastes of the time and was, in Baum's own words, "an immediate success."[2] The play traveled from Baum's Opera House in Gilmour, Pennsylvania, to the Grand Opera House in Syracuse and on to the Windsor Theatre in New York, where it played for a week to packed houses.

For the next six months, the show toured the United States and Canada, going through Toronto, Rochester, Columbus, Milwaukee, and Chicago. While Baum enjoyed his time on the road and the success of his play, there was a part of him that was eager to return home: Baum had met a girl, one who was destined to be the one and only love of his life.

MARRIAGE

Her name was Maud Gage. Frank's sister Harriet, convinced that Maud would be a good match for her brother, arranged for them to meet at a party held by their Aunt Josephine. It was Josephine who officially introduced the two, saying:

> "This is my nephew, Frank. Frank, I want you to know Maud Gage. I'm sure you will love her."
>
> "Consider yourself loved, Miss Gage," was [Frank's] smiling acknowledgement of the introduction.
>
> "Thank you, Mr. Baum," she replied as she held out her hand. "That's a promise. Please see that you live up to it."[3]

Did you know...

L. Frank Baum's mother-in-law, Matilda Joslyn Gage (March 24, 1826–March 18, 1898), was a fascinating woman in her own right: a tireless worker for women's rights, founder of the Women's National Liberal Union, and editor of *The Liberal Thinker*. She was also an outspoken advocate for the rights of Native Americans, an ardent abolitionist, and a freethinker: a woman who spoke out for the rights of the oppressed at a time when very few did so.

She was also the author of such works as *Women, Church and State: A Historical Account of the Status of Women Through the Christian Ages*, a summation of her belief that the kind of patriarchal, male-oriented Christianity then often practiced oppressed women. The book also discusses her beliefs in "good witches," women who "through [their] own wisdom, penetrated some of the most deeply subtle secrets of nature."[*] She goes on to say that to her, "Magic simply means knowledge of the effect of certain natural, but generally unknown laws; the secret operation of natural causes . . . consequences resulting from control of the invisible powers of nature, such as are shown in the electrical appliances of the day, which a few centuries since would have been termed witchcraft."[**]

It is obvious that Gage's beliefs in magic and in the rights of women, and her depiction of an ideal matriarchal (female-ruled) society, had a profound effect on Baum, who brought Gage's vision to life in his world of Oz.

---

[*] Katherine M. Rogers, *L. Frank Baum: Creator of Oz*. St. Martin's Press: New York, 2002, p. 53.

[**] Ibid.

In this circa 1890 engraving, the noted American women's rights advocate, writer, and editor, Matilda Joslyn Gage, is pictured. As Baum's mother-in-law, she would greatly influence his thinking on a wide variety of issues.

That kind of assertiveness was uncommon in a girl of her time, but Maud Gage was far from a common girl. Her mother, Matilda Joslyn Gage, was a nationally known feminist and advocate for human rights; her father, Henry Hill Gage, was a successful dry-goods merchant. The two raised her to be an independent, well-educated girl. She had attended a boys' high school in Syracuse and at the time of her introduction to Frank Baum was enrolled in Cornell University, where her courses included literature, oratory, French, Latin, geometry, physiology, theory of equations, and botany.

The couple had their first date on Christmas Eve 1881. But Maud had other men vying for her affection, and Baum had a theatrical company to run. Yet whenever he had spare time during the summer of 1882, Baum would return home, borrow a horse and buggy from his father, and drive out to the Gage family home in Fayetteville to court Maud. The couple soon fell in love.

There was just one problem: Matilda Gage thoroughly disapproved of the match. Her daughter was well brought up and educated, and Matilda felt that she could do far better than marrying a traveling actor whose career seemed to change with alarming regularity. Nevertheless, Frank Baum knew what he wanted, and one day, sitting in the Gage family's front parlor, he proposed.

Maud said yes and asked Frank to wait a minute while she told her mother, who was sitting in the back parlor. Even though Maud closed the sliding doors between the rooms, Frank could still hear every word of what the two women said. He later reported their conversation:

> I heard Mrs. Gage say: "I won't have my daughter be a darned fool and marry an actor." Maud snapped back: "All right, mother, if you feel that way about it, good bye." "What do you mean, good bye?" Mrs. Gage demanded. "Well," Maud replied, "you just told me I would be a darned fool to marry an actor, and you wouldn't have a daughter of yours do that. I'm going to marry Frank, so, naturally, you don't want a darned fool around the house." Then Mrs. Gage laughed and

said: "All right, Maud. If you are in love with him and really determined to marry him, you can have your wedding right here at home."[4]

Matilda Gage, who had raised her daughter to think for herself, obviously could do nothing else but respect her daughter's decision to marry the would-be actor.

Baum and his mother-in-law quickly came to an understanding. Few people were able to resist his charms, and in time, she grew to respect his ambitions and talents. On November 9, 1882, L. Frank Baum and Maud Gage were married in the front parlor of her family's home and honeymooned at the fashionable resort town of Sarasota Springs, New York.

It was then back to work. Much to her mother's regret, Maud dropped out of college to join her husband with the touring company of *The Maid of Arran*. It must have been difficult adjusting to a life on the road and living in "dreadful" hotels, but she survived. The moment that she discovered that she was pregnant, however, she insisted that life on the road was over and that it was time for them to settle down. Baum hired a new actor to take his place, and the happy couple moved into a rented house in Syracuse, New York, where their first child, Frank Joslyn Baum (known as Frank Jr.), was born in December 1883.

FAMILY AND WORK

The Baums quickly settled into a period of domestic bliss and financial instability. Frank was, for a time, able to support his family on the continued earnings from the still-touring *Maid of Arran* and took the opportunity to write several other plays, none of which were ever performed.

When *The Maid of Arran*'s tour finally ended, Baum was able to use his family's oil business to support his own family. In July 1883, just before the birth of Frank Jr., Baum had opened a store that sold various types of lubricating oil. After Baum's Uncle John, who was also his business manager, became ill in late 1884, Baum was forced to hire a business manager. It soon became evident that the bookkeeper was mishandling the business. On top of that, a fire in Gilmour destroyed not only Baum's theater but also all the costumes and props for *The Maid of Arran*. In order to recover from these twin financial disasters, Baum sold all of his real estate holdings, as well as the production rights to *The Maid of Arran*.

He was, however, able to bounce back. His brother, Benjamin, had invented an improved kind of lubricating oil, and he organized a new company, Baum's Castorine Company, to manufacture and distribute it. Frank was asked to be the company's superintendent, a position he held from 1884 to 1888. Part of his job responsibility seemed to be as a salesman; during this time Frank was often on the road, marketing the product to owners of hardware and drug stores.

It was a good thing Frank had the position with Baum's Castorine Company, because his second son, Robert Stanton Baum, was born in 1886. After Robert's birth, Maud Baum was seriously ill for some time. For several months she was confined to her bed and was attended by a special nurse. She did recover, though, and quickly returned to her role as head of the Baum household.

Neither Frank nor Maud seemed to feel obliged to assume the then-traditional roles of the husband in charge and the wife as his obedient mate. It was obvious to everybody both inside and outside the family that Maud was the head of the house, with control of the finances. Frank, with his naturally sweet and easygoing temperament, was happy to go along.

One family story, recounted by Frank Jr. in his biography of his father, *To Please a Child*, illustrates his parents' relationship. It is a story known as "the affair of the Bismarks." (Bismarks are a kind of filled doughnut.) One fateful day, Frank, anxious to please his children, brought home a dozen Bismarks. His wife, however, wanted to know if he disliked the food she prepared. With a smile, Baum told his wife that while he enjoyed her meals, he also loved having Bismarks for breakfast.

With that, she dutifully served them to him every morning, even though on the third morning he told her that they were going stale; she said that since he had purchased the doughnuts, he would have to eat them.

The Bismarks continued to appear on the breakfast table for the next three mornings. Frank tried hiding them, first wrapping them in newspaper, and then burying them in the ground, but to no avail: Maud continued to serve them. When Frank finally got up the nerve to protest, he said, "Let's stop this nonsense. Those things are unfit and you know it." She responded: "You bought them without consulting me, so you will have to eat them. I'm not going to have food wasted. But, I'll let you off this time if you will promise never again to buy *any* food unless I ask you to get it." [5]

Baum agreed, and the Bismarks affair came to an end. But as Frank Jr. noted: "[I]t had taught him a lesson he never forgot. . . . Around the house she was the boss." [6]

It should come as no surprise, then, that in the Baum household, Maud was the disciplinarian. On one occasion when Robert was very young, he threw the family cat out

Here, Baum's younger sons, Kenneth (left) and Harry, are pictured. Baum had a trunk filled with costumes and wigs, which the boys used for dress up and playacting.

of the house's second-story window. The cat was not hurt, but as Robert remembered it, his mother

> to teach me a lesson, caught me up and held me out the window pretending that she was going to drop me. But it was quite real to me and I screamed so loudly that the neighbors all rushed out and were quite horrified at the spectacle of my

mother dangling me out of the window, not sure but that she would let me drop.[7]

Frank Baum was incapable of such behavior. On one occasion, when called upon to spank his youngest son, Kenneth, Baum became so upset that he was unable to eat his dinner and later apologized to Kenneth. In the Baum household, if anybody was going to punish the children, it was Maud. Her husband was simply too sweet-natured and willing to see the best in people to do anything but comfort and encourage them.

Many years later, Frank Jr., writing in the newsletter the *Baum Bugle*, remembered his father as someone who

> never looked on the dark side of life; never said an unkind word
> about any person; never swore or told a dirty story. His sunny
> disposition, quizzical smile and kindly twinkle in his gray eyes,
> coupled with irrepressible optimism helped all who knew him
> to see their troubles in a different and less important light.[8]

L. Frank Baum would have special need of that optimism in 1887, as the family's financial situation took a sudden and unexpected turn for the worse.

A CHANGE BECOMES NECESSARY

This time, it was the Baum family fortune that began to crumble. After Frank's father, Benjamin Baum, had left the United States to live in Germany, his brother Benjamin became seriously ill and died in February 1886. The father returned from Germany for his son's funeral to discover that the family's businesses were being badly managed. He tried to do what he could, but he died in 1887, unable to stop the downward financial spiral.

In the spring of 1888, Frank Baum returned home from a road trip selling Castorine products. When he went to his office, he made a horrific discovery. The company clerk, who had been managing the business while he was on the road, had shot himself after gambling away the firm's business capital. There was nothing left to do. Frank Baum was forced to sell what remained of the family's businesses, including his opera houses, and to consider his next step.

Like many other Americans of his generation, he looked west and saw opportunity there. In the Dakota Territory, gold had been discovered in the 1870s, and new towns were quickly springing up as pioneers flocked to the area. Maud Baum's own brother Clarkson, her two sisters, and many others from the Syracuse area were among the territory's settlers, establishing the town of Aberdeen where two railroad lines crossed. It seemed an ideal location for the Baums, a place where the family could make a fresh start.

L. Frank Baum visited Aberdeen in June 1888. *The Aberdeen Daily News* considered his visit worthy of report, which mentioned his latest fascination:

> L. Frank Baum of Syracuse, New York, who has been visiting his in-laws here finds recreation from the cares of an extensive business in the fascinating pursuit, amateur photography. Mr. Baum is proficient in the art and during his stay in the city secured a number of fine negatives of Dakota land and cloud scapes.[9]

What did Baum find in Aberdeen? It was in many ways a typical frontier town. With a population of just 3,000 people, Aberdeen was composed of stores, hotels, and banks located on Main Street. Although the streets were not paved, there were raised wooden sidewalks. There was both telegraphic and electric service; houses were lit by gas; there were even some telephones. The newly arrived pioneers from Syracuse, nearly 40 in all, had also done what they could to make their lives more livable. There were lectures, amateur theatrical productions, and musical shows, all performed in the local "Opera House." For Baum, the possibilities that Aberdeen offered made a move appear to be the ideal solution to his financial difficulties.

When he returned home, he wrote to his brother-in-law to discuss the business opportunities in Aberdeen. He believed that there was a potential market for an upper-end variety store, "a Bazaar, selling fancy goods, sporting goods, outdoor games . . . amateur photograph goods, fancy willowware, cheap books and good literature, stationery, toys and crockery specialties, velocipedes . . . etc."[10] On September 20, 1888, Frank, Maud, and their two sons arrived in Aberdeen, hopeful and eager to start their new lives.

DAKOTA TERRITORY

On September 25, 1888, readers of the *Aberdeen Daily News* were treated to the announcement that Baum's Bazaar would be opening on Main Street on October 1, offering "a magnificent and complete assortment of Art Pottery and decorated Table Ware, Bohemian and Native Glass Ware, Parlor, Library and table Lamps, Baskets and Wicker Ware, Toys in immense variety, Latest novelties in Japanese Goods, Plush, Oxidized Brass and Leather Novelties, Gunther's Celebrated Chicago Candies."[11] One week later, the paper noted that nearly 1,000 people attended the store's opening and praised Baum for the beautiful displays of his wares.

On October 12, Baum himself announced that he was now in the possession of a "new poetry grinder," which contributed the following verses after turning the crank:

> At Baum's Bazaar you'll find by far
>
> The finest goods in town
>
> The Cheapest, too, as you'll find true
>
> If you'll just step around . . . [12]

Business at Baum's Bazaar started slowly but gradually picked up. In the meantime, Baum became an important citizen in the town by helping to organize and sponsor the Aberdeen Baseball Club and the professional baseball team, the Hub City Nine; organizing a bicycle club; and performing in amateur theatricals. He also undoubtedly raised eyebrows when he and his wife participated in séances that attempted to contact and speak with the spirits of the dead.

Once again, financial misfortune affected the Baums. For two years running, 1888 and 1889, the area suffered from severe drought. Since the town's economy was based on agriculture, demand for the "luxury" items at Baum's Bazaar dried up. Businesses in Aberdeen began to fail, and the bazaar itself teetered on the verge of bankruptcy. The kindhearted Baum found it impossible not to allow his friends and customers to purchase items on credit. By the end of the year, 161 customers were on the books as owing him money.

With the birth of his third son, Harry Neal Baum, on December 17, 1889, financial pressure continued to grow on Baum. The next month, the bank foreclosed on his shop. Once again, Baum found himself without a job and without a means to support his family. Unwilling to give up on Aberdeen, Baum used what little capital he had to purchase the weekly *Dakota Pioneer*, one of Aberdeen's seven weekly papers. (There were two daily newspapers as well. This was a common situation in the West. Papers were used to advertise town sites as well as to publish legal notices regarding ownership of land.) After renaming the paper the *Aberdeen Saturday Pioneer*, Baum published its first issue on January 25, 1890.

It was a return to his childhood days of the *Rose Lawn Home Journal*. The paper was a one-man operation: Baum purchased some illustrations and articles from a news service, wrote the rest of it, sold advertisements, set the type, and ran the printing press.

The *Aberdeen Saturday Pioneer* was eight pages long; Baum generally wrote a quarter to a half of an issue's content. He reviewed local theatrical productions and amateur musical performances; wrote the social column describing such things as who went to which parties and who was sick; and wrote three to five editorials per issue.

It is through these editorials that we get a glimpse of Baum's concerns at that time. He was a strong supporter of women's rights, due perhaps to the influence of his wife and mother-in-law, and he wrote eloquently about the need for women to have the right to vote. He also discussed his interest in nontraditional religion, his opposition to traditional organized churches, and his personal belief in theosophy (literally "god-wisdom")—and its teaching that every religion has a portion of the truth and is an attempt to help human beings to evolve to greater perfection.

While many of the opinions Baum expressed in his editorials are not surprising to modern readers, two editorials he wrote about Native Americans are a different matter. These editorials, written shortly after the killing of Sioux Indian

Chief Sitting Bull and the later massacre of the remnants of his tribe at Wounded Knee, both expressed his approval of exterminating any remaining Indians. One example, published on December 20, 1890, five days after the killing of Sitting Bull, said in part:

> With his fall the nobility of the Redskin is extinguished, and what few are left are a pack of whining curs who lick the hand that smites them. The Whites, by law of conquest, by justice of civilization, are masters of the American continent, and the best safety of the frontier settlements will be secured by the total annihilation of the few remaining Indians.[13]

These two editorials were the exception in a lifetime of support for minorities. What provoked Baum on these two occasions? Nobody knows for certain, but the common fear among settlers of Indian attacks was likely one factor. In 2006, two of Baum's descendants apologized to the Sioux nation for any hurt that their ancestor may have caused.

MRS. BILKINS

By far, however, the most popular feature in the *Aberdeen Saturday Pioneer* was Baum's fictional creation "Mrs. Bilkins," the author of a column called "Our Landlady." In the column, Baum, writing as "Mrs. Bilkins," the owner of a local boardinghouse, gave "her" opinions on everything from local gossip to political topics to women's rights to life in the modern world. Through Mrs. Bilkins, Baum was able to express some of his more unconventional opinions in an amusing manner. For example, while Baum believed that it was a perfectly acceptable idea that a woman could be mayor of Aberdeen, few others of the time would have agreed. Mrs. Bilkins, on the other hand, could announce that *she* planned to run for mayor, thereby making Baum's point for him.

Mrs. Bilkins, whose speech was written in an uneducated dialect, also gave Baum the opportunity to speak in wonder of the new machines and technologies that were springing up around them. In one column, Mrs. Bilkins describes a visit to a farm where she saw an unusual wagon. "I rubbed my eyes in amazement for a minit," she tells her boarders, "'cause there was no hoss or beast o' any kind hitched to it."[14] She went on to explain that the wagon was powered by electricity and that machines could perform all the work needed to be done on the farm: cook dinner, set the table, and even wash the dishes!

For the first few months of the paper's existence, it prospered, so much in fact that it expanded to 12 pages. Baum was optimistic about both his and the paper's future. But, after the elections of 1890, when nearly every candidate and cause he supported, including the right to vote for women, was defeated, Baum seemed to lose interest in the paper. Hard times once again took their toll as well, as a sharp drop in the price of wheat forced many local residents to move. With the birth of his fourth and last child, Kenneth Gage, on March 24, 1891, Baum was no longer able to hold on.

The next month, after two and a half years of hard work, Frank Baum was once again forced into bankruptcy, or, as he said, "I decided the sheriff wanted the paper more than I did."[15] He had failed again and was without a job or a means to support his wife and four sons. Now 35 years old and without a real career, he knew that something had to be done to get his life and finances in order. But what?

Pictured, the Administration and Electrical buildings at the 1893 World's Columbian Exposition in Chicago, Illinois. While living in Chicago, the Baum family went to see the exposition's exhibits as often as they could.

Struggles and a New Beginning

IN MAY 1891, L. Frank Baum went to Chicago, Illinois, in search of work. It was an obvious choice. As America's second-largest city, Chicago was not only a major commercial center but had become home to an increasing number of artists, writers, and publishers. And, with the planned World's Columbian Exposition of 1893, the largest world's fair ever to be held, it was a city on the rise.

Baum was certain that his experience running a newspaper in Aberdeen would help him find newspaper work in Chicago. Competition was fierce, however, and he applied to the city's major papers, without success. Finally, a new paper, the

Chicago Evening Post, hired him as a reporter and editorial writer for just $20 a week—a small salary even by the standards of the time. Although it was not much to support a family on, it was a start.

Two weeks later, Maud and the kids, now between seven years and five months old, arrived in Chicago to live in the house that Baum had rented. It was a simple cottage, without running water, a bathroom, or even a connection for a gas hookup. The family was to live there for four years.

When one is making such a small salary, every penny counts. So imagine Baum's despair when, upon receiving his first paycheck from the *Post*, he saw that it was a dollar and a half less than he expected. Due to a misunderstanding, his pay was $80 a month, not $20 a week. Baum was angry. Maud was even angrier. Since it was impossible for him to support his family on that wage, Baum left newspaper work in the fall to take a job at the Siegel, Cooper & Company department store as a china buyer.

Although the salary was low, the work was pleasant, and Baum soon met executives at the major china wholesale houses, including the sales manager of Pitkin and Brooks, a company that sold china and glassware throughout the Midwest. Learning of an opening, Baum jumped at the chance to try his hand at working for Pitkin and Brooks as a traveling salesman, giving up the security of a steady salary for the chance to earn even more money by working on commission.

Like most salesmen just starting out, business was slow. Years later, his son Robert wrote in the *Baum Bugle*: "Money was not very plentiful and a penny went a long way. Red letter days were when father would come home from a sales trip and we would ask for a penny and he would magnanimously hand out a nickel."[1] Times were so tough that Maud was forced to work as well, giving lessons in embroidery and lace making. Maud did so well that by February 1897 she had more than 20 students and had earned enough money to buy both furniture and a new rug for their house.

Gradually though, Baum, through persistence, drive, and imagination, became his firm's leading salesman. He taught his customers how best to show the china in their stores and helped to create imaginative window displays to help bring customers in. On one occasion, according to his son Harry, he went well beyond the usual window display for a hardware store: "He wanted to create something eye-catching, so he made a torso out of a wash boiler, bolted stovepipe arms and legs to it, and used the underside of a saucepan for the face. He topped it with a funnel hat, and what would become the inspiration for the Tin Woodman was born."[2]

By 1895, Baum was doing so well that the family was able to move to a better house with a bathroom and gaslights. A maid from Sweden was also imported to help clean house and take care of the younger boys. Baum could even afford to take his entire family to see the wonders of the world's fair. A complete city had been built and designed for the occasion, where new machines and technology were on display. Electric power—still a novelty to most people—was a main attraction. The fair was completely lit by electric lights; and in the Electricity Building a model home included such new inventions as an electric stove, washing machine, carpet sweeper, doorbell, and lighting fixtures. Two of Thomas Edison's latest inventions were on display as well: a new and improved phonograph and a new machine called the Kinetoscope, an early movie machine.

It was an amazing spectacle that became known as the White City. The Baum family went as often as they could, and it seems likely that the fair's beauty, as well as its innovative technology, must have played a part in inspiring the Emerald City of Oz. As Katherine M. Rogers points out in her biography of Baum: "Its fountains, domes, minarets, spires and fluttering banners suggested the architecture of the Emerald City. Lit by hundreds of electric lights, the White City could have suggested a jeweled city to Baum."[3]

Did you know...

Theosophy is a doctrine of religious philosophy and metaphysics that originated with Helena Petrovna Blavatsky. Frank and Maud Baum had long been intrigued by Madam Blavatsky's ideas, and on September 4, 1892, the couple was admitted to the Ramayana Theosophical Society in Chicago.

Baum found spiritual comfort in the belief that all religions are attempts to help humanity to achieve spiritual perfection; that the world we see is part of many we do not see; that life on Earth is just one step in our spiritual progression; and that the good (or evil) we do during one's time on Earth influences one's next stage of return, or reincarnation. Indeed, Frank and Maud Baum were convinced that they had met in earlier reincarnations, and they often attended séances in the hope of finding proof that spirits and the afterlife truly existed.

Despite the family's increased financial security, nobody in the Baum family was particularly happy about how it was attained. Frank's work was difficult, involving both constant travel (a source of unhappiness for Baum himself, who was devoted to his home and family) and the intense physical labor of packing, unpacking, and repacking six to 10 trunks with samples of china and glassware. And, of course, since his income was dependent on what he sold, his finances were in a constant state of flux.

The pressure of being a traveling salesman began to affect Baum's health, and he suffered from increased chest pains and strain on his heart. After a doctor suggested he find less stressful work, Baum once again found himself at the end of the road. If his health could not stand the stress of life on the road, what could he do?

Inspiration came to him from a somewhat unlikely source: his mother-in-law. Matilda Joslyn Gage had begun to spend her winters living with the Baums, despite her lingering disapproval of Baum's seeming inability to settle down into a steady career and properly support his wife and children. Even his success as a traveling salesman was not enough to satisfy her. She knew that he was unhappy doing it and that his family was also unhappy.

But there was one thing about L. Frank Baum that earned her unwavering approval: his ability to tell stories. Baum was known throughout the neighborhood as a master storyteller, and on many evenings, the local children could be found sitting at his feet, listening to his imaginative tales and yarns. On cold nights, the whole group would pop popcorn or pull taffy; in the summer there was homemade ice cream to be cranked in an ice-cream freezer. It was such a regular event that every night at 9:00 P.M., the local policeman would come to the Baums' door to walk the children safely home.

Many times, Baum would read the children the rhymes of Mother Goose. But when he did, his listeners often had questions for him: Why, they asked, would the mouse run up the clock? How could four and twenty blackbirds survive being baked in a pie? How could someone live in a pumpkin shell? How could someone live in a shoe? Baum was forced to come up with stories to help explain the nursery rhymes, and it was those stories that captured his mother-in-law's imagination.

She decided that Baum's talent lay in these stories, in creating fantasies for children, and she urged him to put his stories down on paper and send them to a children's book publisher. At first, Baum could not imagine that anyone outside of family and friends would be interested in his stories. But his wife, Maud, who generally had the last word, disagreed. "Mother is nearly always right about everything," she told him.[4] Thus, he had no choice. By June 1893, L. Frank Baum had two publishers interested in his first book. He had taken the first step in the long road to fame and success as the country's leading author of children's books.

FIRST BOOKS

While Baum waited for a decision from the two publishers, he tried getting his work published elsewhere. He worked as a freelance journalist and wrote short poems and stories, but he had a hard time getting them accepted. Baum became so dejected at his lack of success that he began keeping an account book that he called his "Record of Failure" to keep track of his numerous rejections.

Eventually, though, the *Chicago Times-Herald* published some of his poems and stories, as well as editorials on women's rights. He also took the opportunity to start a new trade journal aimed at window dressers called *The Show Window: A Journal of Practical Window Trimming for the Merchant and the Professional*, to help store owners arrange their window displays in a more eye-catching and appealing manner. The journal did well, which helped to ease Baum's financial concerns. Those concerns were further eased when Way & William Publishers agreed to publish Baum's first children's book, *Mother Goose in Prose*.

When the book was published in 1897, it featured illustrations by a new artist from Philadelphia, Maxfield Parrish, who would go on to have a long and distinguished career as a painter and an illustrator. One can only imagine Baum's happiness and pride when, at the age of 41, he was able to hold his first published book in his hands. Naturally, he presented his wife with a copy, which he lovingly autographed for her: "One critic I always fear and long to please. It is my Sweetheart . . . I hope this book will succeed, for her sake, for we need the money success would bring. But aside from that sordid fact I care little what the world thinks of it. The vital question is: What does my sweetheart, my wife of fifteen years, think of it?"[5]

The book, while not a blockbuster, sold well enough that the publisher agreed to publish Baum's second book, *Phunnyland*, the next year. Unfortunately for Baum, Williams went out of business before that could happen.

WORKING WITH DENSLOW

It was at the Chicago Press Club that Baum was introduced to William Wallace Denslow, who had earned his reputation as a poster artist and was as well known for his trademark signature (which included a seahorse) as he was for his huge mustache. He and Baum hit it off immediately, and when Baum showed Denslow the poems for children he had written over the years, Denslow thought they had the makings of a fine children's book. The two agreed to work together and found a publisher for their work in early 1899.

The book started with a simple concept. Mother Goose had become so busy with her Women's Club activities that it was up to her husband, Father Goose, to entertain the children with *his* songs and rhymes. The author and artist worked together closely on the book: Baum sometimes changed his words to match Denslow's drawings, while Denslow used Baum's words to reach new heights of comic illustration.

In one instance, when Baum told Denslow that he had written a rhyme about an "ostrich dance," Denslow came up with a drawing of an ostrich dancing alongside a little girl wearing ostrich plumes. But, since Baum's original idea for the poem was about a man who moved *like* an ostrich, Baum quickly dropped it and wrote a new poem to match Denslow's drawing:

> Have you seen little Sally
>
> Dance the Ostrich Dance?
>
> The dainty way she does it
>
> Will surely you entrance.
>
> With the left foot here,
>
> And the right foot there,
>
> And the ostrich feathers waving
>
> In her golden hair;

She's surely very charming—

You'll see it at a glance—

When little Sally dances

In the Ostrich dance.[6]

Indeed, one of the most important aspects of the book is the way that the illustrations are not just "illustrations" but work together *with* the poems to make the book a unified whole—a new phenomenon in children's books. One problem this caused for the author and illustrator was that the extensive use of color illustrations made the book tremendously expensive to publish. The two agreed that they would pay for the illustrations themselves and would supply "all the [printing] plates for the pages, cover, and even advertising posters."[7] Baum, still hurting financially, was forced to borrow the money to pay his half of the expenses. It was a gamble, but one that he was willing to take.

The gamble paid off. Published in September 1899, *Father Goose: His Book* was an immediate success. By Christmas, it had sold 75,000 copies, making it the best-selling children's book of the year. Critics loved the book as well, with the *Times-Herald* saying that there is "a quaint funniness about this book . . . the oldest and wisest heads will read it and laugh till the tears trickle," and *The Home Magazine* noting, "Many of Mr. Baum's verses will linger in the minds of the little ones and cling to them, probably, when they are old and gray."[8]

With the success of *Father Goose*, Christmas 1899 was a particularly happy one for the Baum family. (The only unhappy spot might have been that the reviewers tended to praise Denslow's illustrations more than Baum's verses.)

The original front cover of L. Frank Baum's Father Goose: His Book *is pictured. When the book was first published in 1899, it became the best-selling children's book of the year.*

But then, as son Harry wrote later as an adult, Frank Baum always made Christmas special for his family:

> We always had a Christmas tree, and this was purchased by Father and set up in the front parlor behind drapes that shut off the room. This, Father explained, was done to help Santa Claus, who was a very busy man, and had a good many houses with children to call upon.

Santa Claus (Father) came a little later to deck the tree, and we children heard him talking to us behind the curtains. We tried to peek through cracks in the curtains, but although we could hear Santa Claus talking, we never managed to see him, and only heard his voice. On Christmas Day, when the curtains were opened, there was the Christmas tree that Santa Claus had decorated—a blaze of different colors, and the presents for each of the boys stacked below it![9]

On one especially memorable Christmas, the Baums had four Christmas trees—one for each of the boys—set up in each of the four corners of the room!

By summer 1900, Baum was doing so well from the sales of *Father Goose* and from the continued success of his journal *The Show Window*, that the family was able to move into a big two-story house on the northwest side of Chicago, send Frank Jr. to the Michigan Military Academy (a surprising move given Baum Senior's own dislike of military school), and even to rent a summer cottage at a Michigan resort town, Macatawa Park.

The cottage became a treasured family getaway, a way to escape the city's summer heat for the beach and cool breezes of Lake Michigan. Baum named the cottage the Hyperudenbuttscoff, painted the name on a sign, and hung it outside the cottage, where it drew puzzled looks and questions about what the word meant. Baum got the word from a Chicago museum exhibit, where it was used to refer to the skeleton of a whale, but the Baum family used it to describe anything that was hard to describe.

Because Baum still had to work in Chicago editing *The Show Window*, he lived in the city during the week while the family spent the summer of 1899 summering at Macatawa, and then he took the ferry to Macatawa on weekends. The Baums quickly became the organizers of fun for the beach

community: Maud started card clubs, while Frank organized a water carnival and began a weekly talent show.

Baum also enjoyed the occasional cigar, holding it unlit
in his mouth. The only time he actually lit up was when he
went swimming. "You see," he explained, "I can't swim,
so when the cigar goes out I know I'm getting over my
depth."[10]

A FULL-TIME WRITER

In October 1900, Baum announced that he was resigning
as editor of *The Show Window*: "The generous reception
. . . of my books for children, during the last two years, has
resulted in such constant demands upon my time that I find
it necessary to devote my entire attention, hereafter, to this
class of work."[11]

Indeed, by this time Baum had published six children's
books. In addition to *Mother Goose in Prose* and *Father
Goose: His Book*, he privately published a collection of
poetry, as well as sold *By the Candelabra's Glare*; *The
Army Alphabet*; *The Navy Alphabet*; and his long-delayed
Adventures in Phunnyland, now called *A New Wonderland*,
to publishers. If *Mother Goose* showed the practical side
of Baum, with his concern for explanation and making
children's stories believable, *A New Wonderland* showcased
his imaginative side. It was his first attempt to create a
complete fantasy world out of his own imagination. In it,
he describes a land where a king is able to escape from a
deep hole by turning it upside down; where a donkey is one
of the kingdom's wisest creatures because he has eaten all
the schoolbooks; and where a wicked wizard steals the toes
of a princess.

His next novel would combine the two parts of Baum,
creating a perfectly logical, yet utterly imaginative and

fantastic world, while at the same time giving the world a uniquely American fairy tale. As Baum writes in the book's introduction,

> The time has come for a series of newer "wonder tales" in which the stereotyped genie, dwarf, and fairy are eliminated, with all the horrible and blood-curdling incident devised by their authors to point a fearsome moral to each tale. . . . [The book] was written solely to pleasure children of to-day. It aspires to being a modernized fairy tale, in which the wonderment and joy are retained and the heart-aches and nightmares are left out.[12]

In this groundbreaking novel, Baum would use everything he had learned about children, writing, and life—his experiences in Aberdeen, South Dakota, the use of illusion in creating window displays, and his mother-in-law's discussions of witches, magic, and the power of women. Yet, little did L. Frank Baum know that this book would be his biggest success to date, one that would establish him, at the age of 44, as America's most important children's book author.

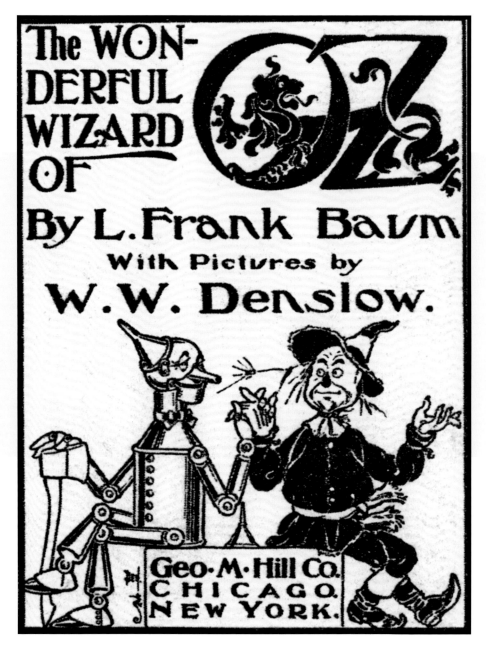

This is the title page illustration by W.W. Denslow from the first edition of The Wonderful Wizard of Oz, *the first book in Baum's enormously successful Oz series.*

5

The Wonderful Wizard of Oz

Dorothy lived in the midst of the great Kansas prairies, with Uncle Henry, who was a farmer, and Aunt Em, who was the farmer's wife. Their house was small, for the lumber to build it had to be carried by wagon for many miles. . . . When Dorothy stood in the doorway and looked around, she could see nothing but the great gray prairie on every side. Not a tree nor a house broke the broad sweep of flat country that reached the edge of the sky in all directions.[1]

—L. Frank Baum

THE BOOK, of course, was *The Wonderful Wizard of Oz*. Published in April 1900, it was, as Baum later told his brother, the best thing he had ever written.

For several years, Baum had been developing the ideas that went into *The Wonderful Wizard of Oz* through the stories he told the neighborhood children. He then began writing down the stories as "The Emerald City," writing in pencil in handwriting so neat that the book was eventually typeset from his own longhand copy. (Baum kept the pencil with which he finished the book, framed it, and eventually hung it on the wall of his study in Hollywood with the simple label "With this pencil I wrote the MS. of '*The Emerald City.*' Finished Oct. 9th, 1899.")

Once again, the book was a collaborative effort with artist W.W. Denslow. After Baum had done a fair amount of work on the manuscript, he showed it to Denslow. The two men would then meet to discuss the book; Denslow would sketch the characters, which, in all probability, then influenced Baum as he continued to develop the book.

When the book was close to completion, the partners took it to Hill Publishing Company, which agreed to publish the book under the same agreement as it had *Father Goose*: Baum and Denslow would supply the plates for the 100 illustrations and 24 color plates and Hill would pay all the other costs. Baum and Denslow would share the 12 percent royalty payments, with each receiving nine cents for every copy sold at the list price of $1.50. But Hill was unhappy with their proposed title "The Emerald City," which changed to "From Kansas to Fairyland," to "The Land of Oz," before the book went to print with its final title: *The Wonderful Wizard of Oz*.

The book tells the story of Dorothy, a young girl living in Kansas with her Uncle Henry and Aunt Em. When a "cyclone" (technically a tornado) lifts up her small house with Dorothy still in it, it carries her and her dog Toto to the Land of Oz, dropping her right on top of the Wicked Witch of the East, killing her immediately. As anyone who has seen the beloved 1939 movie knows, the plot takes Dorothy to the Emerald City, the capital city of Oz, to ask the Wizard who lives there to send her home. Along the way she makes friends who accompany her on her journey (a scarecrow who wants a brain, a tin man who desires a heart, and a lion in search of courage) to the Emerald City, and then, at the Wizard's request, on to the West to kill the Wicked Witch who rules that part of the country.

After killing the witch and returning to the Emerald City, Dorothy and her friends learn that the Wizard is not really a wonderful wizard after all, but a fake, a "humbug" from Kansas. The Wizard, after giving Dorothy's friends what they wanted (but really possessed all the time), promises to take Dorothy home to Kansas himself in a balloon. But after the balloon leaves without Dorothy, she is forced to go with her friends to visit Glinda, the good witch of the North, who tells her that all she has to do is to click her

Did you know...

Where did L. Frank Baum come up with the name "Oz" in the first place? According to his son Frank Jr., the name Oz came to his father one day when he was telling a group of children a story about Dorothy, the Scarecrow, and the Tin Woodman. When one of the children asked him where all those adventures were taking place, Baum looked over at his file cabinet, noticed that the last drawer was labeled O–Z, and replied "Oz!"

child within whom he remembered so well. He wanted to entertain.[5]

In her biography of L. Frank Baum, Katherine Rogers elaborated on one of the things that made Baum such a special writer—his ability to write about children from a child's perspective:

> In *The Wizard*, Baum first perfected the tone that distinguished all his best fantasies, a tone that is authentically childlike without sinking into simple-mindedness. He entirely avoided self-conscious adult mannerisms such as writing down from a position of superior sophistication or conjuring up the mysterious, poetic atmosphere that adults assume is appropriate to fantasy. Instead, he told his story as a child would experience it, grounding it in a child's understanding of reality. Both Kansas and Oz are presented in a matter-of-fact way; Dorothy takes things as they come, without speculating about them; she reacts, interprets, and judges with a small child's simplicity. Baum retained enough of his childish self to give him wonderful insight into children's understanding and feelings.[6]

It is this combination of matter-of-factness alongside of fantastical characters and worlds that makes Baum unique and brings a distinctively American style to his work.

POPULARITY AND NEW VENTURES

The Wonderful Wizard of Oz, not surprisingly, became the best-selling children's book of 1900. Initially, Baum did not even know just how well the book was doing. But as Christmas approached that year, Maud needed money for presents and told Frank to ask his publisher for an advance (payment for books that had not yet been sold). Dutifully, Baum went to visit his publisher, George Hill, at his office, promising to ask for $100.

When Hill learned why his prize author was visiting, he authorized a check to be drawn for all the money owed to Baum at that point. Baum stuffed the check in his pocket without looking at it, certain that it would not be for much. When he arrived home, he handed the check directly over to Maud, as promised. Imagine his surprise when the check was not for $100, but for $3,432.64. Maud was so excited at their unexpected success that she burned the shirt she was ironing at the time!

Despite his success Baum, as always, had more than one iron in the fire. In 1901, the following year, he published a total of three children's books: *Dot and Tot of Merryland*, *American Fairy Tales*, and *The Master Key: An Electrical Fairy Tale*. It is interesting to note that none of these are Oz books. When Baum wrote the first Oz book, he had not thought of it as being the first book in a series but as a single book that had reached its logical conclusion.

The first of these books, *Dot and Tot of Merryland*, tells the tale of Dot, the daughter of a wealthy banker, who goes to stay at Roselawn, an estate that bears a remarkable resemblance to Baum's own beloved childhood home. There she meets Tot, the gardener's son, and the two of them go off in a boat on the river and through a tunnel to Merryland, where they encounter the Queen of Merryland, a large wax doll. The book, while successful in creating a lovely fantasy world, is considered by many critics to be one of Baum's weakest, due to its lack of real plot.

American Fairy Tales is a collection of stories that Baum originally published in newspapers between March and May 1901. In them, he attempted to Americanize the fairy tale, not as in *The Wonderful Wizard of Oz*, by making fairylands seem oddly familiar, but by moving the traditional elements of fairy tales, namely magic and fairies, into American settings. It was a largely unsuccessful experiment. Why, as Katherine Rogers pointed out, is it plausible, for example, that an old trunk in the attic of a house in Chicago would contain three Italian bandits who escaped the moment that the trunk was opened and proceeded to rob the place?

On the other hand, *The Master Key: An Electrical Fairy Tale, Founded on the Mysteries of Electricity and the Optimism of its Devotees. It was Written for Boys, but Others May Read It* is one of Baum's most intriguing books, and one worthy of rediscovery. In this science fiction novel for teenagers, Baum tells the story of Rob, who, like his own son Rob, was constantly shaking up the house with his electrical experiments. And, just as in the Baum household, while the fictional Rob's mother is fed up with his experiments, his father, as Baum writes,

> was delighted with these evidences of Rob's skill as an electrician, and insisted that he be allowed perfect freedom in carrying out his ideas.
>
> "Electricity," said the old man sagely, "is destined to become the motive power of the world. The future advance of civilization will be along electrical lines. Our boy may become a great inventor and astonish the world with his wonderful creations."
>
> "And in the meantime, said the mother, despairingly, "we shall all be electrocuted, or the house burned down by crossed wires."[7]

One day though, in the course of his experiments, Rob touches the "Master Key of Electricity" and accidentally summons the Demon of Electricity, who must obey Rob's commands and provide him with three electrically powered gifts per week for a total of three weeks. Among his gifts, the Demon provides Rob with an electrical wristwatch that allows him to fly; a box of tablets, each of which provides him with enough nutrition for an entire day; a small box that shows him anything that is happening anywhere (somewhat like a television); and a Character Marker, a pair of eyeglasses that will reveal to Rob the real character of anyone he is looking at.

Rob, like any teenage boy, at first is thrilled with the gifts and powers given to him by the Demon, but when Rob is offered an Electro-Magnetic Restorer that will cure disease and restore the dead back to life, he refuses to accept it and returns all the Demon's other gifts. Rob tells the Demon that he is not ready for such powers: "I'm not wise enough. Nor is the majority of mankind wise enough to use such inventions as yours unselfishly and for the good of the world. If people were better, and every one had an equal show, it would be different."[8]

As Katherine Rogers points out, *The Master Key* is typical Baum in that it illustrates the link between magic and technology. In Oz, magic is often seen as an advanced form of technology; in the United States, advances in technology can have the appearance of magic. And, as in Oz where magic is best used only by the wisest of rulers, it also follows that, at least at the time when Baum wrote *The Master Key*, most people were not ready to wisely use or even to understand the potential power of the new technology. Even so, at the end of the book, Rob muses that eventually, perhaps in another century, mankind will be able to use its new technological powers wisely.

The book did well, going through several printings in its first year of publication, and was named by readers of *St. Nicholas*, a popular children's magazine of its day, as one of their favorite books. *The Master Key* was the first of Baum's titles to be published by a new publisher, Bobbs Merrill, a far more prestigious house than Hill. (When Hill went bankrupt, Bobbs Merrill purchased the rights to publish and sell both *Father Goose* and *The Wonderful Wizard of Oz.*)

TO THE STAGE

Although Baum had not yet written a new Oz book, he had not left Dorothy and the Wizard behind. Even though L. Frank Baum and illustrator Denslow had had their differences since the publication of *The Wonderful Wizard of Oz* (Denslow had worked on his own, writing and illustrating *Denslow's Mother Goose* as well as a "Father Goose" comic strip, both of which Baum objected to), they knew that their creative partnership was too strong to give up on. They decided they would write a work for the stage, along with 23-year-old composer Paul Tietjens. It would be up to Baum to write the play itself as well as the lyrics for the songs; Denslow would design the costumes.

Baum's original idea was to write a musical called "The Octopus," referring to political business scandals of the time. Songs were written, but when no producer showed an interest in the musical, the trio switched gears. Baum decided to write a musical based on his own best-selling book, *The Wonderful Wizard of Oz.*

Frank and Tietjens presented the completed musical to Fred Hamlin, the business manager of Chicago's Grand Opera House. Hamlin liked the idea, based in no small part on the fact that his father, who owned the theater, had made his fortune selling a patent medicine called Hamlin's Wizard Oil. Hamlin was certain that his father would get a kick out of seeing the word "wizard" emblazoned in lights on the theater's marquee.

To assist Frank and Tietjens, Hamlin hired Julian Mitchell to direct the show. On Mitchell's recommendation, Baum hired two theatrical experts to help him to transform his musical into a theatrical extravaganza. Gone was the simple show that Baum had envisioned. In its place was a big show laden with visual effects, vaudeville-style comedy routines, and songs that may or may not have anything to with what was actually going on onstage. Indeed, the show's most popular song, "When You Love, Love, Love," had originally been written for "The Octopus."

Despite his misgivings, Baum rewrote the play on the advice of Mitchell and his theatrical advisers. In the new version of the play, Dorothy was no longer the little girl of the book. Instead, she became a young woman, all the better to allow her to have a romance with a newly created character, the poet laureate of Oz, Dashemoff Daily.

Other changes were made. Gone was Dorothy's beloved dog, Toto. In his place was a beloved cow named Imogene. The Scarecrow and the Tin Woodman moved from supporting characters straight to center stage. It seemed all the better, in the mind of the show's producer, to focus attention on the actors playing the roles: the vaudeville comedy team of Fred Stone and David Montgomery. The two comedians enlivened the show by bringing in the comic routines they were known for, regardless of whether or not they had anything to do with the story. By the time the show opened on July 16, 1902, Baum's original story had long since vanished. In its place was "a hodgepodge of spectacular effects, comic romantic entanglements, slapstick routines, puns and wisecracks."[9]

Despite the changes, the show was a spectacular success that seemed to give audiences of the time exactly what they wanted. A member of the opening night audience, Max Maier, wrote later:

> The opening scene showed the home of Dorothy Gale. . . . In this serene and peaceful setting the cry "Cyclone" was raised by a dozen farm hands. The stagelights slowly dimmed and in a moment of total darkness, with crashing cimbals [*sic*] and kettle drums, drowning the terrified voices of the actors, I noted the lowering of a white screen from my perch in the gallery. I cannot say by what magic the illusion of a full-fledged cyclone in action was produced. Still vivid is my recollection of many flying objects, barns, houses, cattle, poultry, and people.[10]

The combination of song and dance, familiar humor, spectacular special effects, and a chorus line of girls in tights made the show a huge hit. Chicago critics loved it as well, with the *Daily News* calling it spectacular and adding, "Money fairly drips from the gorgeous walls and skies of the Emerald City and the land of the Munchkins and from the costly robes of the pretty girls and amazing atmospheres of silver mists and golden lights."[11]

The show ran in Chicago for 14 weeks, playing to standing-room-only crowds of 185,000 and grossing $160,000—huge figures for that time. The show then went on the road, going west, then into Canada, then returning to Chicago for another two-week run before opening in New York City's Majestic Theatre in January 1903.

New York reviewers panned the show, but audiences could not get enough of it. It played in New York for 293 nights, making it the biggest hit of the decade. After the show's New York run ended, it continued to tour the country for the next eight years. It was by any standards a huge hit and made all concerned with the show wealthy. It is estimated that Baum earned between $90,000 and $100,000 from the stage version of *The Wonderful Wizard of Oz*, more than enough, it seems, to ease any unhappiness he may have felt about the changes he was asked to make in the show. He was finally able to buy his family the things he felt they deserved: bicycles, a motorboat, even their first car, a Ford.

The success of the show also influenced his next book. If *The Wonderful Wizard of Oz* could be transformed into a moneymaking theatrical event, why couldn't another? His next book would be a return to Oz and one written both to capitalize on the play's success as well as to lay the basis for another play in the future. The Oz series was about to begin.

An early twentieth-century picture postcard showing the Hotel del Coronado, in Coronado Beach, California, where Baum and his family often vacationed during the winters. While at the hotel, Baum wrote numerous books.

Back to Oz

THE INITIAL PUSH for a new Oz book came from Baum's new publisher, Reilly & Britton, which had been formed by two former employees of Baum's first publishers, Hill and Company. Because the Scarecrow, due to his abundance of brains, assumes the Wizard's position as ruler of the Emerald City at the end of *The Wonderful Wizard of Oz*, the sequel was tentatively titled "His Majesty the Scarecrow," before changing to "Further Adventures of the Scarecrow and the Tin Wood-man" to capitalize on the success of the theatrical production of *The Wizard*, before *finally* becoming *The Marvelous Land of*

Oz. (But even that title was shortened after publication to *The Land of Oz.*)

Interestingly, the new book is missing the first book's main character, Dorothy. As a result of her absence, there is no contrast displayed between the fantasy world of Oz and the great outside world; all of the novel's action takes place within Oz itself. Even so, Baum continued to display his gift of making his fantastic characters seem utterly realistic by his selection of carefully thought-out details. The Scarecrow cannot pick up a pill with his stuffed hands; the Tin Woodman cannot unscrew a box because of his stiff fingers. And one of the book's most important elements, the magical Powder of Life, is packaged in an old pepperbox with its label carefully drawn in pencil.

The hero of *The Land of Oz* is Tip, who is being raised by a witch named Mombi. As Tip runs away from her in search of adventure, the reader is reintroduced to old friends such as the Scarecrow and the Tin Woodman and also meets new ones such as Jack Pumpkinhead and the Saw-Horse, who are brought to life by the Powder of Life, which Baum describes in loving detail. Other new characters, such as H.M. Woggle-Bug, T.E. (H.M. for Highly Magnified and T.E. for Thoroughly Educated), are introduced, as Tip flees Mombi and runs across an army of women whose goal is to overthrow the Scarecrow and seize power for themselves. Finally, though, all of the book's main characters end up at the palace of Glinda the Good Witch, whose role throughout the series is to fix everything and tie up each book's numerous loose ends.

What is revealed at the end of the book still has the power to raise eyebrows. Tip, it seems, is not really a boy at all. He is instead the Princess Ozma, the rightful ruler of Oz, who had been changed by Mombi into the boy Tip. When Glinda informs him that he must be changed back into a girl, he naturally objects, before finally giving in, telling Glinda: "I might try it for a while,—just to see how it seems, you know. But if I don't like being a girl you must promise to change me into a boy."[1] Glinda informs him that it is not possible, so after the final transformation, Tip tells his assembled friends: "'I hope none of you will care less for me than you did before. I'm just the same Tip, you know; only—only—' 'Only you're different!' said the Pumpkin-head; and everyone thought it was the wisest speech he had ever made."[2]

Tip's transformation into the Princess Ozma is just one more sign that Baum was a feminist who thought that girls were at least equal to boys—an uncommon belief for an American man living in his time. (It should be noted, of course, that throughout *The Land of Oz* Baum mocks the army of women led by General Jinjur. It seems likely, however, that the army is in the novel only so that the later theatrical version could turn them into an attractive chorus line. Throughout the book, it is clear that Baum has written *The Land of Oz* with the express idea of turning it into a play at a later date.)

The book, illustrated by 26-year-old artist John R. Neill, was published under the full title *The Marvelous Land of Oz: Being an Account of the Further Adventures of the Scarecrow and Tin Woodman and Also the Strange Experiences of the Highly Magnified Woggle-Bug, Jack Pumpkin, the Animated Saw-Horse and the Gump* on July 5, 1904, to excellent reviews. Praising the book's invention and humor, a reviewer for *The Cleveland Leader* noted that the book works "because Mr. Baum himself believes in his work and delights in it. . . . A man must have the child heart to write for children. This does not imply that his intellect should be childish."[3] The reviewer added that "part of the book, and that the least enjoyable, has been written with a view to the stage. General Jinjur and her soldiers are only shapely chorus girls."[4]

In his "Author's Note" for *The Land of Oz*, Baum claimed he wrote the sequel because "I began to receive letters from children, telling me of their pleasure in reading the story and asking me to 'write something more' about the Scarecrow and the Tin Woodman."[5] Yet, given the fact that he dedicated the book to the actors who played the Scarecrow and Tin Woodman in the stage show, combined with the obvious theatrical elements written into the text, it is no wonder that shortly after the book's publication, he went to work transforming his book into a theatrical extravaganza titled *The Woggle-Bug*.

It was a spectacular failure. When the show opened at the Garrick Theatre in Chicago on June 18, 1905, the *Tribune* said that it was "only a shabby and dull repetition of the cheapened *Wizard of Oz*. The book is the weakest portion of the new offering. It contains virtually no story whatever and witty lines are almost lacking."[6] The show closed on July 13, just three weeks later.

The show's failure was a humiliation for Baum, but fortunately, he had not invested any of his own money in the production. For the next three years, Baum's energy was devoted to writing fiction for children, teens, and even adults. The money earned from his previous books, along with those from the still-running *Wizard of Oz* stage show, gave him financial freedom. In addition to keeping the family house in Chicago and their cottage in Macatawa, the Baums also spent several months of each year traveling.

In 1904, for example, the Baums traveled through the American Southwest by automobile. Of course, it was a different kind of travel than what we are used to today: There were as yet no highways, no AAA maps to let drivers know where they are going, nor even any roadside hotels. Roadside camping was not an uncommon occurrence, and a good day's travel meant going 60 miles!

Although much of the journey involved "roughing it," the Baum family ended their trip in the lap of luxury at the Hotel del Coronado located across the bay from San Diego. Built in 1877, the hotel was (and remains) one of America's premier beach resorts, an all-wooden Victorian structure that throughout the years has hosted royalty, celebrities, and presidents. Baum fell in love with the place, telling an interviewer that "those who do not find Coronado a paradise have doubtless brought with them the same conditions that would render heaven unpleasant to them did they chance to gain admittance."[7]

The Baums returned often to spend winters at the hotel, and it was there that Baum worked on many of the books he completed in the early 1900s. Among them were his *Animal Fairy Tales*, traditional fairy tales featuring talking animals that are based on the question: "Why should not the animals have their own Fairies as well as mortals?"[8] *The Enchanted Island of Yew* is one of the rare works of Baum that takes place in the past. It tells the story of a fairy, bored with her life, who gets transformed into a boy, Prince Marvel, to experience a series of adventures with bandits, dragons, and evil magicians, all with that typical Baumian comedy touch. For example, the Royal Dragon of Spor, suffering from rheumatism, is unable to breathe fire because his inner flame has gone out and his keepers have run out of matches!

Among this group of non-Oz books, most critics consider *Queen Zixi of Ix* to be the best. Many, in fact, think that it is his best story, period, and Baum himself thought it was the best book he had ever written. The plot focuses on a magic cloak made by fairies to assist helpless mortals. Among the elements of the story are children abused by their guardian; a witch who tries to steal the cloak; villains who tyrannize people; and the loss of the magic gift when it is not properly used. As Baum critic Michael O. Riley writes of *Queen Zixi of Ix* in his book *Oz and Beyond: The Fantasy World of L. Frank Baum*:

> All the adventures are integrated into the plot; there are no visits to exotic countries or encounters with strange charac-ters that have no relation to the story. Even Baum's recurring themes are well integrated: the fairies wove the cloak because they were bored and dissatisfied with their usual, never-ending occupations, and Queen Zixi's longing for what she cannot have precipitates the working out of the plot. Zixi herself is Baum's most nearly tragic character; she must learn to live with the knowledge that what she is inside is very different from what she appears to be.[9]

OTHER SERIES, OTHER VOICES

In addition to publishing Baum's original novels and col-lections of stories, Baum's publisher, Reilly & Britton, also published series books for children that followed the same characters through different settings and adventures. Baum, always anxious to earn more money and to keep busy, began writing several of these series himself.

Unlike his own works, he did not write them under his own name. L. Frank Baum was reserved for his fairy tales, which were regularly published each Christmas—just in time for holiday gift giving. These new series would be written under pen names like Suzanne Metcalf and Laura Bancroft, who wrote books for young children; Captain

Hugh Fitzgerald, who wrote action stories for boys; and Schuyler Staunton, who wrote adventure stories mixed with romance for adults.

Baum achieved his greatest success as a series writer as Edith Van Dyne, writing a successful series of books aimed at teenage girls. The contract for the first book illustrates the unusually casual relationship between Baum and his publishers, as well as the lack of seriousness with which his publisher conceived the series:

> Baum shall deliver to The Reilly and Britton Co. on or before March 1, 1906, the manuscript of a book for young girls on the style of the Louisa M. Alcott stories, but not so good, the authorship to be ascribed to "Ida May McFarland," or to "Ethel Lynne" or some other mythological female.[10]

The contract goes on to say "that in case Baum shall at any time become hard up" they would give him an advance of his royalties "upon demand any sum or sums of money that he may wish to squander that will not total more than two thousand dollars, although they hope it will be less."[11]

The first book "by" Edith Van Dyne, *Aunt Jane's Nieces*, is the story of Jane Merrick, a cantankerous old woman who is about to die. She asks her three nieces, none of whom she has met, to come visit her so she can determine to which of the three she will leave her money. All three of the girls are poor, but they have very different personalities. The case of who should receive the money quickly becomes irrelevant when Aunt Jane dies and it is discovered that she really had no money to leave anybody. Fortunately, Jane's long-lost brother, who had moved in with Aunt Jane, is rich, and he decides to support all three of the girls.

The subsequent books in the series follow the girls through their adventures growing up. Many of their stories are taken directly from Baum's own life: In *Aunt Jane's Nieces and Uncle John*, for example, the characters travel through the Southwest and stay at the Hotel del Coronado, just as the Baums did!

So successful was Baum with this series that his earnings rivaled that of the Oz books. And with it, Frank and Maud Baum finally reached the level of financial security for which they had longed. To celebrate, the happy couple made their first trip overseas in January 1906.

They took what was then known as the Grand Tour: five weeks in Egypt, six and a half weeks in Sicily and Naples, three weeks touring northern Italy, then two weeks in

Did you know...

Although Frank Baum thoroughly enjoyed his tour of Egypt and Europe, he did not share his wife's appreciation of the paintings of such masters as Titian, Michelangelo, Raphael, and Leonardo da Vinci. Maud complained in a letter home: "L.F. grieves me. He says 'he can tell me one old master from another as soon as he reads the name on the frame,' and other slighting remarks when I grow enthusiastic."* In Baum's book *Aunt Jane's Nieces Abroad*, Uncle John seems to agree with Baum's assessment; while in Florence, John mocks the famous paintings: "After all, they're only daubs. Any ten-year-old boy in America can paint better pictures."**

* Angelica Shirley Carpenter and Jean Shirley, *L. Frank Baum: Royal Historian of Oz.* Minneapolis: Lerner Publications Company, 1992, p. 90.

** Ibid., p. 91.

Switzerland and France. It was an extraordinary trip, and the two were delighted to learn that Frank's work was known not only in America but also worldwide. In Cairo, for example, on their first night at the famous Shepheard's Hotel, the band greeted them with selections from *The Wizard of Oz* stage show. And at the same hotel, they met a young girl from Algeria, who with her family had recently crossed the desert by camel. For her trip, she had been allowed to bring one book. The book she brought? *The Wonderful Wizard of Oz*!

Upon their return home, both Baums went to work transforming their experience into books. Maud published a collection of the letters she had written to friends and family during the trip under the title *In Other Lands Than Ours*. And Frank placed the action of *Aunt Jane's Nieces Abroad* in Italy. In Sicily, Uncle John is kidnapped and held for ransom. Patsy makes friends with the kidnapper's daughter, who is disguised as a boy, and tricks her into revealing where her father is holding Uncle John. Patsy and Beth then storm the hideout and rescue John, armed with revolvers!

Upon returning home, the Baums took the opportunity to celebrate their twenty-fifth wedding anniversary, surrounded by family and friends. It was Frank who sent out the invitations, which included the following report:

Quarrels: Just a few. Wife in tears. Three times (cat died; bonnet spoiled; sore toe).

Husband swore: 1187 times; at wife, 0.

Causes of jealousy: 0. (Remarkable in an age of manicured men and beauty doctor women.)

Broke, occasionally; bent, often.

Unhappy, 0.[12]

It had been a remarkable 25 years, filled with struggle, doubt, and, finally, happiness and financial security.

DOROTHY GOES BACK TO OZ

In 1907, Frank Baum published a total of six books, but the most highly anticipated work was his annual fairy tale. Ever since the publication of *The Marvelous Land of Oz* in 1904, Baum's publisher, as well as his legions of fans, had been clamoring for a new Oz book. Baum, who for years had resisted returning to Oz, finally gave in, realizing that his greatest success, both popular and critical, was with his Oz books.

The third Oz book, published under the full title, *Ozma of Oz: A Record of her Adventures with Dorothy Gale of Kansas, the Yellow Hen, the Scarecrow, the Tin Woodman, Tiktok, the Cowardly Lion and the Hungry Tiger; Besides Other Good People Too Numerous to Mention Faithfully Recorded Herein*, opened up new possibilities for Baum as an author. As Michael O. Riley notes, with this book, "he totally reversed the meaning and significance of Oz as it had first been created in *The Wizard*. It can be said that *Ozma of Oz* is the real beginning of the Oz series."[13]

What does Riley mean by that? In *Ozma of Oz*, Dorothy, now several years older than she was in *The Wonderful Wizard of Oz*, returns to Oz after a storm at sea washes her overboard. She lands on a beach in Ev, near Oz, accompanied by a yellow hen, Billina. When Billina begins talking, Dorothy knows she is once again at the beginning of an adventure in "fairyland."

Dorothy and Billina find a robot, a mechanical man called Tik-Tok (whose name is also spelled Tiktok). The three meet the dangerous Princess Langwidere, who, instead of changing her appearance with new clothes or with makeup, instead goes to her dressing room and changes heads! Gore Vidal remembers that when he read it as a young boy, he "found the changing of heads fascinating. And puzzling: since the brains in each head varied, would Lang[w]idere still be herself when she put on a new head or would she become someone else? Thus Baum made logicians of his readers."[14]

When Dorothy refuses to give up her head for Langwidere's collection, the Princess locks her up in a tower, where she is rescued by a party from Oz on its way to rescue the Queen of Ev and her children from the wicked Nome King, who is established as the series' top villain. Among the rescue party are Dorothy's old friends the Scarecrow, the Tin Woodman, and the Cowardly Lion, as well as Princess Ozma, who quickly becomes Dorothy's best friend.

The party goes deep into the bowels of the Earth to confront the Nome King, and after many adventures, it is Dorothy and Billina who save the day and rescue the Royal Family of Ev. The Ozians along with Dorothy triumphantly return to Oz, where there are celebrations before Ozma sends Dorothy back to her Uncle Henry with the use of the Magic Belt that Dorothy captured from the Nome King.

The book is one of Baum's most imaginative, but it is more than that. Riley points out:

> In *The Wizard* the strange and beautiful . . . Land of Oz is the place of danger and trial, the ordeal through which Dorothy has to go to reach her goal of home. Baum subtly changed all that in *Ozma*: . . . Oz becomes not the ordeal but the goal, the place of the heart's desire and, in a very real sense, Dorothy's true home because Ozma crowns her a princess of Oz, thus making her a part of that Land. . . .
>
> Once Baum had changed Oz from a place to escape from into a great and good place to be sought, he opened the

way for a whole new kind of development, and Oz became the haven and the goal for almost all his American characters. . . . The problem became not how to leave Oz, but how to reach it; and a new type of plot entered his fantasies—the quest for Oz.[15]

The sickly boy who had spent his childhood reading and dreaming of other worlds had created an ideal one of his own, one that helped him achieve literary immortality.

The next book in the series, *Dorothy and the Wizard in Oz*, follows a similar pattern. This time Dorothy and her companions have to reach Oz from a land far underground, where they arrive after falling through a hole formed by an earthquake. Encounters with odd creatures such as the emotionless vegetable people known as the Mangaboos, a reunion with the onetime Wizard of Oz himself, and other exciting adventures follow. Finally, Princess Ozma, checking in with Dorothy through her Magic Mirror, brings Dorothy and her friends back to Oz, before sending Dorothy once again back home. (The Wizard, forgiven for being a "humbug," decides to stay in Oz, where he becomes one of Ozma's most trusted advisers.)

DISASTER

L. Frank Baum was now the author of three highly successful series: the Oz books for children, the Aunt Jane's Nieces books for teenage girls, and the Boy Fortune Hunters books for teenage boys. He and Maud, after years of tough times, were now able to maintain a very comfortable lifestyle, one far out of reach for many writers. Baum, however, being Baum, was not completely satisfied in remaining *just* a children's book author. The theater, as always, beckoned, so Baum came up with the idea of presenting the Oz books onstage. This time, though, there would be no chorus girls. It would be Baum's own stories for children. And Baum himself would be the star.

The show was called *The Fairylogue and Radio-Plays*. Baum financed the shows himself, borrowing funds from his close friend Harrison Rountree. The show was unlike anything ever seen on the stage—combining short films (still in their infancy), slides, and live actors—all held together by the narrator, L. Frank Baum. Unlike an ordinary travelogue, the *fairylogue* (a word coined by Baum himself) meant a trip to fairyland. The word radio in the title referred not to radio as we know it but instead the process invented by Michel Radio to hand-color the movies, which were filmed in black and white.

The show premiered in Grand Rapids, Michigan, on September 24, 1908, and traveled throughout the Midwest and the East before closing in New York City on December 31. By all accounts, the show was visually impressive, and audiences appreciated what Baum was attempting to do. Unfortunately for Frank and Maud Baum, the expensive show lost an enormous amount of money.

Baum's costs to put on the show were extraordinary: Films made in Chicago studios had to be sent to France to be hand-tinted, 114 slides had been made, and 27 musical numbers had been composed by Nathaniel Mann. Actors and an orchestra had to be hired and paid, equipment moved from city to city, and theaters hired. Instead of making him rich, as he had hoped, the show had lost Baum his financial security. He found himself heavily in debt to his friend Harrison Rountree. He and Maud would have to start again to rebuild their lost fortune.

Pictured, the cover of the 1915 novel The Scarecrow of Oz, *a sequel in the Oz series and one of Baum's personal favorites.*

7

The Royal Historian of Oz

IN DIRE FINANCIAL straits, Baum returned to Oz in *The Road to Oz*, considered by many to be one of the weakest books in the series, at least in terms of plot. In it, Dorothy and Toto find themselves lost in a new fairyland. While trying to get back to Oz, they become friends with a tramp know as the Shaggy Man, a lost boy named Button-Bright, and the rainbow's daughter, Polychrome. When they arrive in Oz (after many adventures, of course), they learn that it was Ozma herself who sent them on their way to get them to the Emerald City in time for her birthday party! The party, of course, is attended by all of the most prominent members of fairyland, including characters from

Baum's other books such as Queen Zixi of Ix, the Queen of Merryland, and even "the most Mighty and Loyal Friend of Children, His Supreme Highness—Santa Claus!"[1]

It is interesting to note that *The Road to Oz* reflects Baum's ongoing money concerns by making Oz a place where money itself has no value. When the Shaggy Man tells the Tin Woodman that his new place must have cost a lot of money, the Tin Woodman replies,

> "Money! Money in Oz! . . . What a queer idea! Did you suppose we are so vulgar as to use money here?"
>
> "Why not?" asked the shaggy man.
>
> "If we used money to buy things with, instead of love and kindness and the desire to please one another, then we should be no better than the rest of the world. . . . Fortunately money is not known in the Land of Oz at all. We have no rich, and no poor; for what one wishes the others all try to give him, in order to make him happy, and no one in all Oz cares to have more than he can use."[2]

Unfortunately for Frank and Maud Baum, they did not live in Oz. Despite the success of *The Road to Oz*, Baum's finances continued to be troubled. He ran up debt in Chicago, forcing him and Maud to sell their summer cottage in Macatawa and move to a rented house in Los Angeles, California. Eventually, on August 1, 1919, Baum, unable to pay his debts to Rountree, signed over to him the copyrights and royalties to all of his books published by Bobbs Merrill, including his most popular work, *The Wonderful Wizard of Oz*, as well as nine others until all his debts were paid. Baum would never earn another dime from those books.

Facing financial ruin, Baum was forced to ask his current publishers, Reilly & Britton, for an advance on his next Oz book; they instead agreed to pay him a monthly salary. Even with a steady income, Baum could not make ends meet. On June 11, 1911, he filed for bankruptcy, listing assets of just two suits, 11 reference books, and a typewriter. How could this be? Fortunately for Frank, Maud had stepped in months earlier and transferred the title to the family assets and the royalties from Reilly & Britton into her name. The bankruptcy court could not touch them.

Among the assets listed in her name was the Baum family's new house, Ozcot, built on a large lot in what was then the small suburb of Hollywood, using money inherited from her mother. It was a beautiful home with four bedrooms, a study, a long porch with views of the mountains, living room, kitchen, library, sunroom, and enough land for a garden, archery range, and chicken yard. Frank Baum would live in this house until the day he died.

ALWAYS A WRITER

Despite the distraction of his ongoing financial difficulties, Baum continued to write steadily. What else could he do? There were new Aunt Jane's Nieces books to be written as well as books for the other series. And, perhaps most important, there was the sixth Oz novel to be written, *The Emerald City of Oz*, which he intended to be the final book in the series.

It is one of his very best. In this book, the Nome King attempts to tunnel under the Deadly Desert surrounding Oz and into the Emerald City, where he plans to recapture his Magic Belt and use it to conquer all of Oz. In the meantime, Dorothy, this time accompanied by Aunt Em and Uncle Henry, returns to Oz, this time for good. Once again, new fantastical characters are introduced and exciting adventures are had by all before the Nome King is defeated.

At the book's end, Princess Ozma and Glinda the Good Witch decide that because of the recent invention of airplanes, Oz will soon be overwhelmed by visitors from the outside. To make sure this never happens, Glinda casts a spell that makes the fairyland invisible to the outside world. The novel ends with Dorothy writing a final message to Frank Baum: "You will never hear anything more about Oz, because we are now cut off forever from all the rest of the world. But Toto and I will always love you and all the other children who love us."[3]

With the Oz books behind him (or so he thought), Baum attempted to establish a new series of fantasy books for children. In 1911, he published *The Sea Fairies*, the story of a little girl named Trot and her companion, Cap'n Bill, who are turned into a mermaid and merman so they can travel under the sea. Sales, though, were disappointing, and much to Baum's dismay, the sales for Oz books began dropping as well.

Fortunately, he could still rely on the Aunt Jane's Nieces series, which continued to utilize his own life experiences. In *Aunt Jane's Nieces on Vacation* (1912), for example, the girls start their own newspaper, much as Frank Baum did in Aberdeen so many years earlier. In fact, many of his experiences as an editor appear in the book, including a duel he was forced to fight over a typographical error!

Because Baum was not ready to give up on Trot and Cap'n Bill, he published a sequel in 1912, *Sky Island*, in which the intrepid pair travels by way of a flying umbrella to an island in the sky. To help bolster the novel's popularity, he added two characters from his Oz books, Button-Bright and Polychrome. Even though the book was greatly superior to *The Sea Fairies*, it failed to reach much of an audience, selling even fewer copies than its predecessor—just 11,749 in its first year.

COMMUNICATING WITH OZ

With his other books proving to be unpopular, Baum really had no choice. "The Royal Historian of Oz," as he had become known, could not escape the pleadings of his audience of young readers, his publishers, and undoubtedly his wife as well. He would have to return to the Oz series. But *The Emerald City of Oz* had seemingly shut the door to the possibility of future Oz books. How could he reopen it in a believable manner?

The explanation was given in the introduction to the seventh in the series of Oz books, *The Patchwork Girl of Oz*. In it, Baum informs his readers that a young fan wrote to him and asked if it would be possible to communicate with

Did you know...

Did you know that the pioneering experiment Search for Extraterrestrial Intelligence (SETI) started at Cornell University in 1960 was originally named Project Ozma? The object of the experiment was to search for signs of life in distant solar systems using interstellar radio waves. It was named Project Ozma because it was inspired by Baum's supposed communications by wireless to learn of the events in Oz that take place after *The Emerald City of Oz*, in which Oz is made invisible and cut off from the rest of the world!

Dorothy via telegraph to learn of the latest happenings in Oz. Baum writes that he set up a wireless telegraph tower in his backyard, took lessons in how to use it, and via Glinda the Good Witch, who has a book that records every event that takes place anywhere in the world, gets word to Dorothy, who agrees to communicate with "The Royal Historian" via the Shaggy Man, who is the only person in Oz who knows how to use a telegraph. Ingenious, right?

Works set in Oz once again began to flow from his pen. *The Patchwork Girl of Oz* was followed up by *Tik-Tok of Oz*, which was based on an unsuccessful stage play of the same name. These books, while not selling as well as the previous Oz titles, did well enough that Baum was encouraged to take a chance on a rapidly growing Hollywood business: movies.

Through his membership in the Los Angeles Athletic Club, Baum had become involved with a smaller group within the club—the Lofty and Exalted Order of Uplifters. The group had met for years on a regular basis, putting on short plays and revues for their own amusement. In 1914, some of Baum's friends in the group convinced him to allow them to make movies based on the Oz books. Baum, always fascinated by theater and technology, agreed and became president of the new Oz Film Manufacturing Company.

Fortunately for Baum, he did not invest anything but his time in the new venture, for the company was not a success. Two films, *The Patchwork Girl of Oz* and *The Magic Cloak* (based on *Queen Zixi of Ix*), were completed, but only *The Patchwork Girl* was released. The film, although innovative for its day, failed when audiences decided that it was "just" a children's film. A third and final film, *His Majesty the Scarecrow of Oz*, was also released, but it failed to earn enough money to earn back its costs. By the summer of 1915, the Oz Company had closed altogether, and Baum had lost a year's efforts with very little results. Once again Baum was forced to give up his other interests and return to what it seemed he did best—write children's books.

COMING TO AN END

The next book in the Oz series, *The Scarecrow of Oz*, was one of Baum's personal favorites, but it sold poorly. To make matters worse, Baum's health after finishing the book was also very poor. But he refused to listen to his doctor's advice and continued to eat three heavy meals a day, which led to a new bout of chest pains and an inflamed gallbladder. Despite being in almost constant pain, Baum, in addition to the Aunt Jane's Nieces books, wrote another Oz book, *Rinkitink in Oz*.

Rinkitink in Oz also failed to sell as well as previous Oz books. The Aunt Jane's Nieces series continued to sell, however, as the girls continued to "grow up" and, in *Aunt Jane's Nieces in the Red Cross*, they even went to Europe to serve as nurses in World War I.

Baum refused to give up on the Oz books, though. He saw each new year as an opportunity to recapture his old popularity. *The Lost Princess of Oz* (1917) sold relatively poorly as well. This was a disappointment for Baum, who knew it was one of his most imaginative and tightly plotted works: Someone in Oz has stolen Ozma's magic picture, Glinda's Great Book of Records, and even the Wizard's magic tools—even Ozma herself is missing. It would be up to Dorothy, with the assistance of her friends, to save the day.

In 1918, Baum published *The Tin Woodman of Oz*, which proved both a critical and popular success. In this book, the

In this photo taken on Thanksgiving Day 1918, Maud and Frank Baum (both seated) are surrounded by their family. The author was in failing health at this time.

Tin Woodman pays a visit to his old home, where he was changed from a human being in love with a young girl into a man made out of tin. Before he met Dorothy in the first book, his ax, under the spell of a witch, had chopped off parts of his body one by one, each of which were replaced by a tinsmith in tin. But, since it is the Land of Oz, his old parts do not die, and in one imaginative scene, the Tin Woodman has a conversation with his old head, now being kept in a cupboard.

(Also in the book, the Tin Woodman meets another man made of tin. He had courted the same girl that the Tin

Woodman had, and he, too, had lost the parts of his body to an enchanted ax and was given new parts by the same tinsmith. In another remarkable scene, the two tin men go to visit their old girlfriend, only to discover that she has married a man made up of body parts chopped from both their bodies. In that way, the girl had actually married *both* of them!)

Baum's health was now fading fast, but through sheer force of will, he wrote two additional Oz titles: *The Magic of Oz* and *Glinda of Oz*. Only one of those books would be published in his lifetime. After Baum suffered a stroke on May 5, 1919, both he and Maud knew that he was dying. Even though he could barely speak, he assured his beloved wife that she would be able to keep the house and that the royalties from the books he had worked so hard to write would be enough to support her for many years to come.

The next day, on May 6, L. Frank Baum died. He was in a coma during his last hours, but just before he died, he opened his eyes and said: "Now we can cross the Shifting Sands."[4] He was ready to cross the desert that separated the real world he had always struggled with from the Land of Oz, the magical fairyland of his dreams.

A window-card poster for the original release of The Wizard of Oz, *directed by Victor Fleming. The success of the film—and its annual showing on television starting in the 1950s—sparked a renewed interest in Baum's works.*

A Changing Reputation

THE LAST TWO books of the Oz series were *The Magic of Oz* and *Glinda of Oz*. Based on the popular and critical reaction to those books, Baum's publisher, now called Reilly & Lee, decided that even though its creator had passed away, the series should continue. And, since the publisher agreed that Maud Baum would receive royalties from any new Oz titles, she agreed to let the series continue as well.

The second "Royal Historian of Oz" was noted children's book writer, Ruth Plumly Thompson. She contributed 18 books to the series (four more than Frank Baum himself) before retiring. New writers also added to the series, including illustrator

John R. Neill, Jack Snow, and Rachel Cosgrove. But to Oz purists, it was L. Frank Baum who wrote the only true Oz books.

While Baum's Oz books remained popular with young readers throughout the years, the 1939 movie *The Wizard of Oz* definitely increased interest in Baum's books. But beginning in 1956, what contributed to a resurgence of interest in the works of L. Frank Baum was the film's annual appearances on television. Garnering huge audiences each year, it inspired readers of all ages to once again discover the Land of Oz and its gentle creator, Frank Baum.

Ironically, while his books continued to be discovered by new generations of young readers in the 1940s, 1950s, and even into the 1960s, Baum's reputation with critics and librarians was at an all-time low. Why is that? The author Gore Vidal argues that the books were attacked during this period because of politics. America was then in the midst of the Cold War with the Soviet Union. This continuing state of economic competition, political conflict, and military tension made many people at that time fear any works of literature that gave the reader an opportunity to read about an ideal land far different from the United States. Such alternative worlds were considered somewhat un-American. Passages such as the following from *The Emerald City of Oz* were especially criticized:

> No disease of any sort was ever known among the Ozites, and so no one ever died unless he met with an accident that prevented him from living. This happened very seldom, indeed. There were no poor people in the Land of Oz, because there was no such thing as money, and all property

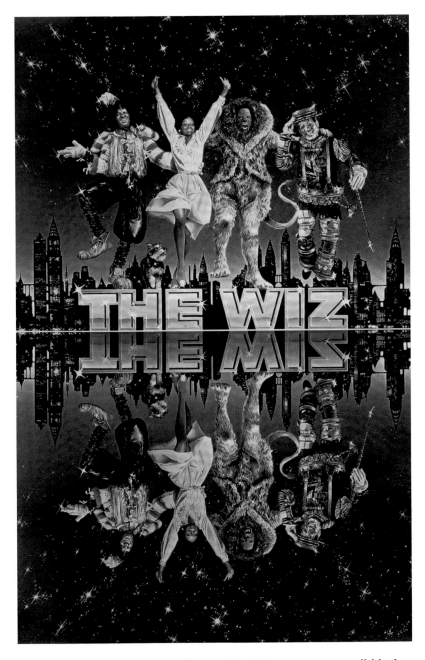

*In the 1978 film **The Wiz**, directed by Sidney Lumet, an all-black cast took on the iconic characters Baum had created. The film had been adapted from the Broadway play of the same name.*

of every sort belonged to the Ruler. . . . Each person was given freely by his neighbors whatever he required for his use, which is as much as any one may reasonably desire. Some tilled the lands and raised great crops of grain, which was divided equally among the entire population, so that all had enough. . . . Each man and woman, no matter what he or she produced for the good of the community, was supplied by the neighbors with food and clothing and a house and furniture and ornaments and games. . . .

Every one worked half the time and played half the time, and the people enjoyed the work as much as they did the play, because it is good to be occupied and to have something to do. . . . So each one was proud to do all he could for his friends and neighbors, and was glad when they would accept the things he produced.[1]

To Baum's critics, the fictional fairyland of Oz was remarkably similar to the "workers' paradise" of Communism, the ideal society preached (but far from practiced) by the leaders of the Soviet Union. In one famous attack, the director of the Detroit Public Library said in 1957 that the Oz books were "of no value" because they encouraged "negativism" and "a cowardly approach to life," and he ordered them removed from the library's children's departments.[2] "There's nothing uplifting or elevating about the Baum series," he insisted.[3]

There were numerous other attacks as well. In 1959, the Florida Department of State issued a paper listing "Books Not Circulated by General Libraries." Topping the list were the Oz books, which were said to be "poorly written, untrue to life, sensational, foolishly sentimental, and consequently unwholesome for the children in your county." The state went on to say that they were "not to be purchased, not to be accepted as gifts, not to be processed, and not to be circulated."[4]

Even as late as 1986, seven families of Christian fundamentalists filed suit against public schools in Tennessee that required the reading of *The Wonderful Wizard of Oz* in elementary school classes. What did they object to? The parents objected to having their children read about witches, as well as the fact that females are treated as equal to men and assume "traditional" male roles in Oz. They even objected to the fact that animals can talk and are treated as humans! The judge went on to rule that the parents could, indeed, remove their children from class when the book was being read.

A CHANGE IN STATUS

Baum had his defenders as well. As early as 1927, Professor Edward Wagenknecht of the University of Seattle called Oz "an important pioneering work."[5] He also recognized Baum's achievement in creating a uniquely American kind of fairy tale, both in its characterizations and in the way that magic is seen in everyday objects and machines. Others soon joined in the chorus of praise for Baum and the Land of Oz. Carol Ryrie Brink, who won the Newbery Medal for her book *Caddie Woodland*, declared: "*The Wizard of Oz* is one of the few great American books for children. It tells a good story in a simple, direct style. It has humor, fantasy, and best of all truth and integrity in the interpretation of human nature."[6]

Over time, that simple statement has gone from being controversial to unarguable. Since the 1960s, Baum's reputation as one of America's greatest storytellers has continued to grow. In the years since his death, Baum has influenced generations of writers who have grown up

In Wicked, *an award-winning Broadway play with music and lyrics by Stephen Schwartz and book by Winnie Holzman that had its debut in 2003, Baum's world is seen through the eyes of the witches of Oz.*

reading the Oz books. Scientists have been inspired by his imagination. And countless numbers of young people, who started their literary journey reading the Oz books, grew up knowing that books could take them places of which they would never have dreamed.

Edward Wagenknecht wrote about the impact that the Oz books had on his life:

> *The Wizard of Oz* opened up to me the whole wonderful, inexhaustible world of literature. . . . [Baum] was preparing me to

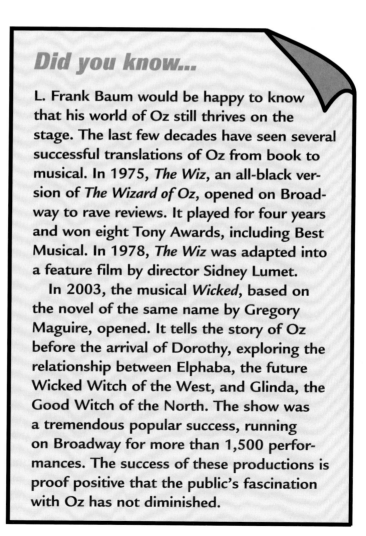

Did you know...

L. Frank Baum would be happy to know that his world of Oz still thrives on the stage. The last few decades have seen several successful translations of Oz from book to musical. In 1975, *The Wiz*, an all-black version of *The Wizard of Oz*, opened on Broadway to rave reviews. It played for four years and won eight Tony Awards, including Best Musical. In 1978, *The Wiz* was adapted into a feature film by director Sidney Lumet.

In 2003, the musical *Wicked*, based on the novel of the same name by Gregory Maguire, opened. It tells the story of Oz before the arrival of Dorothy, exploring the relationship between Elphaba, the future Wicked Witch of the West, and Glinda, the Good Witch of the North. The show was a tremendous popular success, running on Broadway for more than 1,500 performances. The success of these productions is proof positive that the public's fascination with Oz has not diminished.

explore the worlds of other, greater, more difficult writers later on—Dickens and Scott and Shakespeare and Chaucer and Spenser. . . . Perhaps I should have never loved any of them so well if I had not had Baum to show me the way.[7]

Or, as Gore Vidal simply stated, "With *The Emerald City* I became addicted to reading."[8]

It is somehow fitting that L. Frank Baum, who spent his childhood reading and dreaming of better places, would grow up to become the creator of Oz and the author of classic books that have inspired future generations to read and dream of better places. Despite the many ups and downs in his life, once he recognized that his life's calling was to write children's books, he found career happiness, working until nearly the end of his life to write books for the children he loved throughout the world.

It is indeed not surprising that his son's biography of his father was called *To Please a Child*. In his introduction to *Dorothy and the Wizard in Oz*, Frank Baum summed up the happiness he got by writing for children:

I believe, my dears, that I am the proudest story-teller that ever lived. Many a time tears of pride and joy have stood in my eyes while I read the tender, loving, appealing letters that come to me in almost every mail from my little readers. To have pleased you, to have interested you, to have won your friendship, and perhaps your love, through my stories, is to my mind as great an achievement as to become President of the United States. Indeed, I would much rather be your story-teller, under these conditions, than to be the President. So you have helped to fulfill my life's ambition, and I am more grateful to you, my dears, than I can express in words.[9]

Nearly a century after his death, Baum's readers still feel love for the kindly man who wrote *The Wonderful Wizard of Oz*—and grateful that by fulfilling his life's ambition, he brought so much pleasure into their lives.

CHRONOLOGY

1856 Lyman Frank Baum born on May 15 in Chittenango, New York.

1866–1880 After his father gives him a printing press, Baum starts up several newspapers and magazines. He develops a lifelong love of theater.

1881 Baum writes, publishes, and stars in his first successful musical play, *The Maid of Arran*.

1882 Baum marries Maud Gage.

1887–1891 Baum's father dies and the family fortune is lost. Baum and his family move to the small town of Aberdeen in the Dakota Territory, where he operates a store and then runs a local weekly newspaper, *The Aberdeen Saturday Pioneer*.

1891 After the newspaper fails, Baum and his family move to Chicago, Illinois, where he becomes a traveling salesman for a china company. When home, he entertains the neighborhood children with his imaginative stories and tales.

1897 With illustrator Maxfield Parrish, Baum publishes his first children's book *Mother Goose in Prose*.

1899 With illustrator William Wallace Denslow, he publishes *Father Goose: His Book*. The book is a huge success and becomes the best-selling children's book of the year.

1900 *The Wonderful Wizard of Oz* is published, establishing Baum's reputation as a writer.

1902 Baum, in collaboration with Denslow and composer Paul Tietjens, writes a musical stage version of *The Wonderful Wizard of Oz*. Although quite different from the original book, the show is a huge success on Broadway and tours the country for many years.

1902–1908 Baum continues to write children's books both under his own name as well as various pen names, the most successful being Edith Van Dyne. In 1904, he publishes the first sequel in the Oz series, *The Marvelous Land of Oz*.

1908 Baum produces a stage show combining theater, slides, and film, *The Fairylogue and Radio-Plays*. The show is not particularly successful; Baum is forced to declare bankruptcy.

1910 Baum and his family move to Hollywood, California, where they build a home, known as "Ozcot." He continues to write and publish children's books.

1914 Along with several business associates, Baum forms the Oz Film Manufacturing Company. The films, while considered ahead of their time in terms of production values and special effects, fail at the box office.

1915–1919 Although his health is in decline, Baum continues to write books at a steady pace, including one Oz novel each year.

1919 L. Frank Baum dies on May 6. His last book, *Glinda of Oz*, is published posthumously the following year.

NOTES

Chapter 1

1 Aljean Harmetz, *The Making of the Wizard of Oz*. New York: Limelight Editions, 1984, pp. 241–242.

2 Michael O. Riley, *Oz and Beyond: The Fantasy World of L. Frank Baum*. Lawrence, Kan.: University Press of Kansas, 1997, p. 3.

3 Alison Lurie, "The Fate of the Munchkins," *New York Review of Books*. Volume 21, Number 6, April 18, 1974. http://www.nybooks.com/articles/9534.

4 Martin Gardner and Russel B. Nye, eds., *The Wizard of Oz and Who He Was*. East Lansing: Michigan State University Press, 1994, p. 19.

5 Ibid.

Chapter 2

1 Gore Vidal, "The Oz Books," *United States: Essays 1952–1992*. New York: Random House, 1993, p. 1095.

2 L. Frank Baum, *Dot and Tot of Merryland*. New York: The Emerald City Press, 1994, p. 4.

3 Katherine M. Rogers, *L. Frank Baum: Creator of Oz*. New York: St. Martin's Press, 2002, p. 4.

4 Angelica Shirley Carpenter and Jean Shirley, *L. Frank Baum: Royal Historian of Oz*. Minneapolis: Lerner Publications Company, 1992, p. 14.

5 Carpenter and Shirley, *Royal Historian of Oz*, p. 18.

6 Rogers, *Creator of Oz*, p. 3.

7 Rogers, *Creator of Oz*, p. 7.

8 Rogers, *Creator of Oz*, p. 8.

Chapter 3

1 Carpenter and Shirley, *Royal Historian of Oz*, p. 20.

2 Rogers, *Creator of Oz*, p. 10.

3 Carpenter and Shirley, *Royal Historian of Oz*, p. 21.

4 Carpenter and Shirley, *Royal Historian of Oz*, pp. 25–27.

5 Rogers, *Creator of Oz*, p. 14.

6 Carpenter and Shirley, *Royal Historian of Oz*, p. 29.

7 Rogers, *Creator of Oz*, p. 15.

8 Ibid.

9 Carpenter and Shirley, *Royal Historian of Oz*, pp. 31–32.

10 Rogers, *Creator of Oz*, p. 20.

11 Rogers, *Creator of Oz*, p. 23.

12 Ibid.

13 Hastings, A. Waller, "L. Frank Baum's Editorials on the Sioux Nation." http://www.northern.edu/hastings/baumedts.htm.

14 Carpenter and Shirley, *Royal Historian of Oz*, p. 36.

15 Carpenter and Shirley, *Royal Historian of Oz*, p. 39.

Chapter 4

1 Rogers, *Creator of Oz*, p. 48.

2 Carpenter and Shirley, *Royal Historian of Oz*, p. 42.

3 Rogers, *Creator of Oz*, p. 46.

4 Carpenter and Shirley, *Royal Historian of Oz*, p. 45.

5 Rogers, *Creator of Oz*, pp. 62–63.

6 L. Frank Baum, *Father Goose: His Book*. Kessinger Publishing, 2004, p. 11.

7 Rogers, *Creator of Oz*, p. 68.

8 Ibid.

9 Carpenter and Shirley, *Royal Historian of Oz*, p. 52.

10 Carpenter and Shirley, *Royal Historian of Oz*, p. 59.

11 Rogers, *Creator of Oz*, p. 59.

12 Gardner and Nye, *Wizard of Oz*, p. 53.

Chapter 5

1 Gardner and Nye, *Wizard of Oz*, p. 55.

2 L. Frank Baum and Michael Patrick Hearn. ed., *The Annotated Wizard of Oz*. New York: W.W. Norton and Company, p. xliv.

3 Ibid.

4 Ibid.

5 Baum and Hearn, *Annotated Wizard*, p. xlvii.

6 Rogers, *Creator of Oz*, p. 75.

7 L. Frank Baum, *The Master Key*. BiblioBazaar, 2006, p. 11.

8 Baum, *The Master Key*, p. 110.

9 Rogers, *Creator of Oz*, p. 108.

10 Carpenter and Shirley, *Royal Historian of Oz*, p. 65.

11 Carpenter and Shirley, *Royal Historian of Oz*, p. 67.

Chapter 6

1 Vidal, *Essays 1952–1992*, p. 1110.

2 Ibid.

3 Rogers, *Creator of Oz*, p. 127.

4 Ibid.

5 L. Frank Baum, *The Land of Oz*. Mobilreference, Kindle Edition, Locations 1538–1544.

6 Rogers, *Creator of Oz*, p. 130.

7 Rogers, *Creator of Oz*, p. 131.

8 Riley, *Oz and Beyond*, pp. 111–112.

9 Riley, *Oz and Beyond*, pp. 94–95.

10 Carpenter and Shirley, *Royal Historian of Oz*, p. 80.

11 Rogers, *Creator of Oz*, p. 136.

12 Carpenter and Shirley, *Royal Historian of Oz*, p. 92.

13 Riley, *Oz and Beyond*, p. 135.

14 Vidal, *Essays 1952–1992*, p. 1112.

15 Riley, *Oz and Beyond*, pp. 137–138.

Chapter 7

1 Riley, *Oz and Beyond*, p. 159.

2 Riley, *Oz and Beyond*, p. 156.

3 Carpenter and Shirley, *Royal Historian of Oz*, p. 101.

4 Carpenter and Shirley, *Royal Historian of Oz*, p. 121.

Chapter 8

1 L. Frank Baum, *The Emerald City of Oz*. Mobilreference, Kindle Edition, Locations 8552–8565.

2 Baum and Hearn, *Annotated Wizard*, p. xcvii.

3 Ibid.

4 Ibid.

5 Carpenter and Shirley, *Royal Historian of Oz*, p. 134.

6 Baum and Hearn, *Annotated Wizard*, p. c.

7 Riley, *Oz and Beyond*, p. 241.

8 Vidal, *Essays 1952–1992*, p. 1095.

9 L. Frank Baum, *Dorothy and the Wizard in Oz*. Mobilreference, Kindle Edition, Locations 5136–5159.

WORKS BY
L. FRANK BAUM

1873 *Baum's Complete Stamp Dealer's Dictionary*

1886 *The Book of the Hamburgs*

1897 *Mother Goose in Prose*

1898 *By the Candelabra's Glare: Some Verse*

1899 *Father Goose: His Book*

1900 *The Army Alphabet; The Art of Decorating Dry Goods Windows and Interiors; The Navy Alphabet; A New Wonderland; The Wonderful Wizard of Oz*

1901 *American Fairy Tales; Dot and Tot of Merryland; The Master Key: An Electrical Fairy Tale*

1902 *The Life and Adventures of Santa Claus*

1903 *The Enchanted Island of Yew Whereon Prince Marvel Encountered the Hi Ki of Twi and Other Surprising People; The Surprising Adventures of the Magical Monarch of Mo and His People*

1904 *The Marvelous Land of Oz*

1905 *Queen Zixi of Ix, or the Story of the Magic Cloak; The Woggle-Bug Book*

1906 *John Dough and the Cherub*

1907 *Father Goose's Year Book: Quaint Quacks and Feathered Shafts for Mature Children; Ozma of Oz*

1908 *Baum's American Fairy Tales; Stories of Astonishing Adventures of American Boys and Girls with the Fairies of their Native Land; Dorothy and the Wizard in Oz*

1909 *The Road to Oz*

1910 *The Emerald City of Oz; L. Frank Baum's Juvenile Speaker: Readings and Recitations in Prose and Verse, Humorous and Otherwise*

1911 *Baum's Own Book for Children: Stories and Verse from the Famous Oz Books, Father Goose, His Book, Etc., Etc., With Many Hitherto Unpublished Selections; The Daring Twins: A Story for Young Folk; The Sea Fairies*

1912 *Phoebe Daring: A Story for Young Folk*; *Sky Island*

1913 *The Little Wizard Series*; *The Patchwork Girl of Oz*

1914 *Tik-Tok of Oz*

1915 *The Scarecrow of Oz*

1916 *Rinkitink in Oz*; *The Snuggle Series*

1917 *Babes in Birdland*; *The Lost Princess of Oz*

1918 *The Tin Woodman of Oz*

1919 *The Magic of Oz*

1920 *Glinda of Oz*

POPULAR BOOKS

THE EMERALD CITY OF OZ

Originally planned to be the last of the Oz books, it remains one of the finest. The Nome King attempts to conquer Oz but is thwarted in his plans by Dorothy, Princess Ozma, and other illustrious Ozians.

THE LOST PRINCESS OF OZ

One of the most tightly plotted of the Oz books, *The Lost Princess of Oz* recounts what happens in Oz when it is discovered that Princess Ozma, along with the magic tools used by Ozma, the Wizard, and Glinda, are all missing, as is the diamond-studded dishpan used by Cayke, the Cookie Cook.

THE MARVELOUS LAND OF OZ

This is Baum's first return to Oz. It tells the tale of Tip, Jack Pumpkinhead, the Woggle-Bug, the Scarecrow, the Tin Woodman, and the Army of Revolt, and it solves the mystery of what really happened to Princess Ozma of Oz.

QUEEN ZIXI OF IX; OR THE MAGIC CLOAK

This is considered to be Baum's finest non-Oz book. *Queen Zixi* tells the story of a magic cloak, woven by fairies to aid mortals, that is misused by those who wish for things they shouldn't.

SKY ISLAND

In this sequel to Baum's *The Sea Fairies*, Trot and Cap'n Bill, along with the popular Oz characters Button-Bright and Polychrome, use a magic umbrella to visit an island in the sky.

THE WONDERFUL WIZARD OF OZ

This is the book that started it all. Dorothy Gale and her dog, Toto, are carried by a cyclone from Kansas to Oz. There she makes new friends, including the Scarecrow, the Tin Woodman, and the Cowardly Lion. She kills two wicked witches and meets the Wizard of Oz himself.

POPULAR CHARACTERS

DOROTHY GALE

Brave, spunky, and practical, Dorothy has very human responses that allow us to experience the magic and magical characters of Oz.

PRINCESS OZMA

The true ruler of Oz, Ozma had been hidden away, disguised as a boy until Glinda uncovers the truth in *The Marvelous Land of Oz*. Dorothy Gale's best friend, Ozma, rules over Oz with a kind heart, assisted by the Scarecrow, the Wizard, and Glinda.

QUEEN ZIXI OF IX

The heroine of *Queen Zixi of Ix*, Zixi is actually 683 years old but, by magic, appears to be a young girl of just 16. Unfortunately for Zixi, when she looks in a mirror, she sees the old woman she really is—only others see her as a young girl. Zixi hopes to use the magic cloak to make a wish so that she, too, can see herself as young.

THE SCARECROW

Found stuck on a pole in a cornfield by Dorothy, the Scarecrow accompanies her to the Emerald City to ask the Wizard of Oz for a brain. Through the rest of the series, he remains a trusted companion and adviser to both Dorothy and Princess Ozma, and he is the best friend of the Tin Woodman.

THE TIN WOODMAN

Found rusted outside his house by Dorothy, the Tin Woodman accompanies her and the Scarecrow to the Emerald City to ask the Wizard of Oz for a heart. Through the rest of the series, he rules as Emperor of the Winkies, but he is always ready to accompany both Dorothy and Princess Ozma in search of adventure.

THE WIZARD OF OZ

Not really a wizard at all, but a "humbug" born in Omaha, who accidentally arrives in Oz in a balloon and convinces the inhabitants that he is a great and powerful wizard. He returns to America at the end of *The Wonderful Wizard of Oz* but comes back to Oz in *Dorothy and the Wizard in Oz*, where for the remainder of the series he is a trusted adviser to Princess Ozma.

BIBLIOGRAPHY

Baum, L. Frank. *The Annotated Wizard of Oz*. Edited by Michael Patrick Hearn. New York: W.W. Norton and Company, 2000.

———. *Dorothy and the Wizard in Oz*. Mobilreference, Kindle Edition.

———. *Dot and Tot of Merryland*. New York: The Emerald City Press, 1994.

———. *The Emerald City of Oz*. Mobilreference, Kindle Edition.

———. *Father Goose: His Book*. Kessinger Publishing, 2004.

———. *The Land of Oz*. Mobilreference, Kindle Edition.

———. *The Master Key*. BiblioBazaar, 2006.

Carpenter, Angelica Shirley, and Jean Shirley. *L. Frank Baum: Royal Historian of Oz*. Minneapolis: Lerner Publications Company, 1992.

Gardner, Martin, and Russel B. Nye, eds. *The Wizard of Oz and Who He Was*. East Lansing: Michigan State University Press, 1994.

Harmetz, Aljean. *The Making of the Wizard of Oz*. New York: Limelight Editions, 1984.

Hastings, A. Waller. "L. Frank Baum's Editorials on the Sioux Nation." Available online. URL: http://www.northern.edu/hastings/baumedts.htm.

Lurie, Alison. "The Fate of the Munchkins," *New York Review of Books*. Volume 21, Number 6, April 18, 1974. Available online. URL: http://www.nybooks.com/articles/9534.

———. "The Oddness of Oz," *New York Review of Books*. Volume 47, Number 20, December 21, 2000. Available online. URL: http://www.nybooks.com/articles/13918.

Riley, Michael O. *Oz and Beyond: The Fantasy World of L. Frank Baum*. Lawrence, Kan.: University Press of Kansas, 1997.

Rogers, Katherine M. *L. Frank Baum: Creator of Oz*. New York: St. Martin's Press, 2002.

Vidal, Gore. "The Oz Books." *United States: Essays 1952–1992*. New York: Random House, 1993.

FURTHER READING

Fricke, John. *100 Years of Oz: A Century of Classic Images*. New York: Stewart, Tabori & Chang, 1999.

Maguire, Gregory. *Wicked*. New York: ReganBooks, 1995.

Rushdie, Salman. *The Wizard of Oz*. London: BFI Pub., 1992.

Schwartz, Evan I. *Finding Oz: How L. Frank Baum Discovered the Great American Story*. Boston: Houghton Mifflin Harcourt, 2009.

Sunshine, Linda, ed. *All Things Oz: The Wonder, Wit and Wisdom of the Wizard of Oz*. New York: Clarkson Potter Publishers, 2003.

PICTURE CREDITS

INDEX

ABOUT THE CONTRIBUTOR

DENNIS ABRAMS is the author of numerous books for Chelsea House, including biographies of Barbara Park, Nicolas Sarkozy, Jay-Z, Xerxes, Rachael Ray, and Georgia O'Keeffe. He attended Antioch College, where he majored in English and communications. A voracious reader since the age of three, Dennis lives in Houston, Texas, with his partner of 21 years, along with their two cats and their dog, a basenji named Junie B.